PREFACE.

The aim of this book is to indicate how to serve dishes, and to entertain company at breakfast, lunch, and dinner, as well as to give cooking receipts. Too many receipts are avoided, although quite enough are furnished for any practical cook-book. There are generally only two or three really good modes of cooking a material, and one becomes bewildered and discouraged in trying to select and practice from books which contain often from a thousand to three thousand receipts.

No claim is laid to originality. "Receipts which have not stood the test of time and experience are of but little worth." The author has willingly availed herself of the labors of others, and, having carefully compared existing works—adding here and subtracting there, as experience dictated—and having also pursued courses of study with cooking teachers in America and in Europe, she hopes that she has produced a simple and practical book, which will enable a family to live well and in good style, and, at the same time, with reasonable economy.

The absence from previous publications of reliable information as to the manner of serving meals has been noticed. Fortunately, the fashionable mode is one calculated to give the least anxiety and trouble to a hostess.

Care has been taken to show how it is possible with moderate means to keep a hospitable table, leaving each reader for herself to consider the manifold advantages of making home, so far as good living is concerned, comfortable and happy.

M. F. H.

St. Louis, 1876.

SETTING THE TABLE AND SERVING THE DINNER.

An animated controversy for a long time existed as to the best mode of serving a dinner. Two distinct and clearly defined styles, known as the English and Russian, each having its advantages and disadvantages, were the subject of contention. It is perhaps fortunate that a compromise between them has been so generally adopted by the fashionable classes in England, France, and America as to constitute a new style, which supersedes, in a measure, the other two.

In serving a dinner *à la Russe*, the table is decorated by placing the dessert in a tasteful manner around a centre-piece of flowers. This furnishes a happy mode of gratifying other senses than that of taste; for while the appetite is being satisfied, the flowers exhale their fragrance, and give to the eye what never fails to please the refined and cultivated guest.

In this style the dishes are brought to the table already carved, and ready for serving, thus depriving the cook of the power to display his decorative art, and the host of his skill in carving. Each dish is served as a separate course, only one vegetable being allowed for a course, unless used merely for the purpose of garnishing.

The English mode is to set the whole of each course, often containing many dishes, at once upon the table. Such dishes as require carving, after having been once placed on the dinner-table, are removed to a side-table, and there carved by an expert servant. Serving several dishes at one time, of course, impairs the quality of many, on account of the impossibility of keeping them hot. This might, in fact, render some dishes quite worthless.

And now, before giving the details of serving a dinner on the newer compromise plan, I will describe the "setting" or arranging of the table, which may be advantageously adopted, whatever the mode of serving.

In the first place, a round table five feet in diameter is the best calculated to show off a dinner. If of this size, it may be decorated to great advantage, and conveniently used for six or eight persons, without enlargement.

Put a thick baize under the table-cloth. This is quite indispensable. It prevents noise, and the finest and handsomest table-linen looks comparatively thin and sleazy on a bare table.

Do not put starch in the napkins, as it renders them stiff and disagreeable, and only a very little in the table-cloth. They should be thick enough, and, at the same time, of fine enough texture, to have firmness without starch. Too much can not be said as to the pleasant effect of a dinner, when the table-linen is of spotless purity, and the dishes and silver are perfectly bright.

Although many ornaments may be used in decorating the table, yet nothing is so pretty and so indicative of a refined taste as flowers. If you have no *épergne* for them, use a *compotier* or raised dish, with a plate upon the top, to hold cut flowers; or place flower-pots with blossoming plants on the table. A net-work of wire, painted green, or of wood or crochet work, may be used to conceal the roughness of the flower-pot. A still prettier arrangement is to set the pot in a *jardinière* vase.

At a dinner party, place a little bouquet by the side of the plate of each lady, in a small glass or silver bouquet-holder. At the gentlemen's plates put a little bunch of three or four flowers, called a *boutonnière,* in the folds of the napkin. As soon as the gentlemen are seated at table, they may attach them to the left lapel of the coat.

Place the dessert in two or four fancy dessert-dishes around the centre-piece, which, by-the-way, should not be high enough to obstruct the view of persons sitting at opposite sides of the table. The dessert will consist of fruits, fresh or candied, preserved ginger, or preserves of any kind, fancy cakes, candies, nuts, raisins, etc.

Put as many knives, forks, and spoons by the side of the plate of each person as will be necessary to use in all the different courses. Place the knives and spoons on the right side, and the forks on the left side, of the plates. This saves the trouble of replacing a knife and fork or spoon as each course is brought on. Many prefer the latter arrangement, as they object to the appearance of so many knives, etc., by the sides of a plate. This is, of course, a matter of taste. I concede the preferable appearance of the latter plan, but confess a great liking for any arrangement which saves extra work and confusion.

Place the napkin, neatly folded, on the plate, with a piece of bread an inch thick, and three inches long, or a small cold bread roll, in the folds or on the top of the napkin.

Put a glass for water, and as many wine-glasses as are necessary at each plate. Fill the water-glass just before the dinner is announced, unless caraffes are used. These are kept on the table all the time, well filled with water, one caraffe being sufficient for two or three persons. All the wine intended to be served decanted should be placed on the table, conveniently arranged at different points.

At opposite sides of the table place salt and pepper stands, together with the different fancy spoons, crossed by their side, which may be necessary at private dinners, for serving dishes.

Select as many plates as will be necessary for all the different courses. Those intended for cold dishes, such as salad, dessert, etc., place on the sideboard, or at any convenient place. Have those plates intended for dessert already prepared, with a finger-bowl on each plate. The finger-glasses should be half filled with water, with a slice of lemon in each, or a geranium leaf and one flower, or a little *boutonnière*: a sprig of lemon-verbena is pretty, and leaves a pleasant odor on the fingers after pressing it in the bowl. In Paris, the water is generally warm, and scented with peppermint.

Some place folded fruit-napkins under each finger-bowl; others have little fancy net-work mats, made of thread or crochet cotton, which are intended to protect handsome painted dessert-plates from scratches which the finger-bowls might possibly make.

The warm dishes—not *hot* dishes—keep in a tin closet or on the top shelf of the range until the moment of serving. A plate of bread should also be on the sideboard.

Place the soup-tureen (with soup that has been brought to the boiling-point just before serving) and the soup-plates before the seat of the hostess.

Dinner being now ready, it should be announced by the butler or dining-room maid. Never ring a bell for a meal. Bells do very well for country inns and steamboats, but in private houses the *ménage* should be conducted with as little noise as possible.

With these preliminaries, one can see that it requires very little trouble to serve the dinner. There should be no confusion or anxiety about it. It is a simple routine. Each dish is served as a separate course. The butler first places the pile of plates necessary for the course before the host or hostess. He next sets the dish to be served before the host or hostess, just beyond the pile of plates. The soup, salad, and dessert should be placed invariably before the hostess, and every other dish before the host. As each plate is ready, the host puts it upon the small salver held by the butler, who then with his own hand places this and the other plates in a similar manner on the table before each of the guests. If a second dish is served in the course, the butler, putting in it a spoon, presents it on the left side of each person, allowing him to help himself. As soon as any one has finished with his plate, the butler should remove it immediately, without waiting for others to finish. This would take too much time. When all the plates are removed, the butler should bring on the next course. It is not necessary to use the crumb-scraper to clean the cloth until just before the dessert is served. He should proceed in the same manner to distribute and take off the plates until the dessert is served, when he can leave the room.

This is little enough every-day ceremony for families of the most moderate pretensions, and it is also enough for the finest dinner party, with the simple addition of more waiters, and distribution of the work among them. It is well that this simple ceremony should be daily observed, for many reasons. The dishes themselves taste better; moreover, the cook takes more pride, and is more particular to have his articles well cooked, and to present a better appearance, when each dish is in this way subjected to a special regard: and is it not always preferable to have a few well-cooked dishes to many indifferently and carelessly prepared? At the same time, each dish is in its perfection, hot from the fire, and ready to be eaten at once; then, again, one has the benefit of the full flavor of the dish, without mingling it with that of a multiplicity of others. There is really very little extra work in being absolutely methodical in every-day living. With this habit, there ceases to be any anxiety in entertaining. There is nothing more distressing at a dinner company than to see a hostess ill at ease, or to detect an interchange of nervous glances between her and the servants. A host and hostess seem insensibly to control the feelings of all the guests, it matters not how many there may be. In well-appointed houses, a word is not spoken at the dinner between the hostess and attendants. What necessity, when the servants are in the daily practice of their duties?

If one has nothing for dinner but soup, hash, and lettuce, put them on the table in style: serve them in three courses, and one will imagine it a much better dinner than if carelessly served.

Let it be remembered that the above is the rule prescribed for every-day living. With large dinner parties, the plan might be changed, in one respect, *i. e.*, in having the dishes, in courses, put on the table for exhibition, and then taken off, to be carved quickly and delicately at a side-table by an experienced butler. This gives the host time to entertain his guests at his ease, instead of being absorbed in the fatiguing occupation of carving for twelve or fourteen people.

These rules in France constitute an invariable and daily custom for private dinners, as well as for those of greater pretensions. Every thing is served there also as a separate course, even each vegetable, unless used as a garnish. In America and England this plan is not generally liked, although in both these countries it is adopted by many. Americans like, at least, one vegetable with each substantial, a taste, it is to be hoped, that will not be changed by the dictates of fashion. Then, if dishes are to be carved at a side-table, the one-vegetable plan causes the placing of the principal dish on the table before carving to appear more sensible.

When the butler places a dish on the table, and tarries a moment or so for every one to look at it, if it does not happen to be so very attractive in appearance the performance seems very absurd; but when, after putting on the substantial dish, he places a vegetable dish at the other end of the table, his taking the substantial to carve seems a more rational proceeding.

I would suggest, when there is only one dish for a course, which is to be taken off the table to be carved, that the dish should be put on first; then, that the butler should return for the plates, instead of placing the plates on first, as should be done in all other cases.

At small dinners, I would not have the butler to be carver. It is a graceful and useful accomplishment for a gentleman to know how to carve well. At small dinners, where the dishes can not be large, the attendant labor must be light; and, in this case, does it not seem more hospitable and home-like for the gentleman to carve himself? Does it not disarm restraint, and mark the only difference there is between home and hotel dinners?

In "Gastronomie," M. M. believes in a compromise on the carving question. He says, "There were professional carvers, and this important art was anciently performed at the sound of music, and with appropriate gesticulations. We wish our modern gourmands would follow the very good example of Trimalchio in this respect, and, if they must have their viands carved on the sideboard by servants, take care that, like his carvers, they are trained to his art. We shall take the opportunity of entering our protest against an innovation which is going too far. That some of the more bulky pieces, the *pièces de résistance*, should be placed on the sideboard, well and good, though even to this Addison objected, and not without reason; but that the fish and the game should be both bestowed and distributed, like rations to paupers, by attendants, who, for the most part, can not distinguish between the head and the tail of a mullet, the flesh and fin of a turbot, etc., is enough to disturb the digestion of the most tolerant gastronome. We must say that we like to see our dinner, especially the fish, and to see every part of it, in good hands."

Then, again, without paying a high price, one can not secure a waiter who is a good carver. I am almost inclined to say one must possess the luxury of a French waiter for carving at the side-table. English waiters are good. The Irish are generally too awkward. Negroes are too slow. The French are both graceful and expeditious.

Well, what can be done, then, when one has a dinner party, with no expert carver, and the dishes are too large for the host to attempt? I would advise in this case that the dinner should be served from the side. A very great majority of large and even small dinners are served in this manner.

The table, as usual, is decorated with flowers, fruits, etc., but the dishes (*plats*) are not placed upon it; consequently the host has no more duty to perform in the serving of the dinner than the guest. A plate is placed on the table before each person, then the dish, prettily decorated or neatly carved, if necessary, is presented to the left side, so that each person may help himself from the dish. When these plates are taken off, they are replaced by clean ones, and the dish of the next course is presented in like manner. Many prefer to serve every course from the side, as I have just indicated; others make an exception of the dessert, which the hostess may consider a pretty acquisition to the table, while the dish should not be an awkward one to serve.

Some proper person should be stationed in the kitchen or butler's pantry to carve and to see that the dishes are properly decorated. If the hostess should apprehend unskillfulness in carving, the dinner might be composed of chops, ribs, birds, etc., which require no cutting.

There are several hints about serving the table, which I will now specify separately, in order to give them the prominence they deserve.

1st. The waiters should be expeditious without seeming to be in a hurry. A dragging dinner is most tiresome. In France, the dishes and plates seem to be changed almost by magic. An American senator told me that at a dinner at the Tuileries, at which he was present, twenty-five courses were served in an hour and a half. The whole entertainment, with the after-dinner coffee, etc., lasted three hours. Upon this occasion, a broken dish was never presented to the view of a guest. One waiter would present a dish, beautifully garnished or decorated; and if the guest signified assent, a plate with some of the same kind of food was served him immediately from the broken dish at the side-table.

Much complaint has been made by persons accustomed to dinners abroad of the tediousness of those given in Washington and New York, lasting, as they often do, from three to five hours. It is an absolute affliction to be obliged to sit for so long a time at table.

2d. Never overload a plate nor oversupply a table. It is a vulgar hospitality. At a small dinner, no one should hesitate to ask for more, if he desires it; it would only be considered a flattering tribute to the dish.

At large companies, where there is necessarily a greater variety of dishes, the most voracious appetite must be satisfied with a little of each. Then, do not supply more than is absolutely needed; it is a foolish and unfashionable waste. "Hospitality is not to be measured by the square inch and calculated by cubic feet of beef or mutton."

At a fashionable dinner party, if there are twelve or fourteen guests, there should be twelve or fourteen birds, etc., served on the table—one for each person. If uninvited persons should call, the servant could mention at the door that madam has company at dinner. A sensible person would immediately understand that the general machinery would be upset by making an appearance. At small or private dinners, it would be, of course, quite a different thing.

The French understand better than the people of any other nation how to supply a table. "Their small family dinners are simply gems of perfection. There is plenty for every person, yet every morsel is eaten. The flowers or plants are fresh and odoriferous; the linen is a marvel of whiteness; the dishes are few, but perfect of their kind."

When you invite a person to a family dinner, do not attempt too much. It is really more elegant to have the dinner appear as if it were an every-day affair than to impress the guest, by an ostentatious variety, that it is quite an especial event to ask a friend to dinner. Many Americans are deterred from entertaining, because they think they can not have company without a vulgar abundance, which is, of course, as expensive and troublesome as it is coarse and unrefined.

For reasonable and sensible people, there is no dinner more satisfactory than one consisting first of a soup, then a fish, garnished with boiled potatoes, followed by a roast, also garnished with one vegetable; perhaps an *entrée*, always a salad, some cheese, and a dessert. This, well cooked and neatly and quietly served, is a stylish and good enough dinner for any one, and is within the power of a gentleman or lady of moderate means to give. "It is the exquisite quality of a dinner or a wine that pleases us, not the multiplicity of dishes or vintages."

3d. Never attempt a new dish with company—one that you are not entirely sure of having cooked in the very best manner.

4th. Care must be taken about selecting a company for a dinner party, for upon this depends the success of the entertainment. Always put the question to yourself, when making up a dinner party, Why do I ask him or her? And unless the answer be satisfactory, leave him or her out. Invite them on some other occasion. If they are not sensible, social, unaffected, and clever people, they will not only not contribute to the agreeability of the dinner, but will positively be a serious impediment to conversational inspiration and the general feeling of ease. Consequently, one may consider it a compliment to be invited to a dinner party.

5th. Have the distribution of seats at table so managed, using some tact in the arrangement, that there need be no confusion, when the guests enter the dining-room, about their being seated. If the guest of honor be a lady, place her at the right of the host; if a gentleman, at the right of the hostess.

If the dinner company be so large that the hostess can not easily place her guests without confusion, have a little card on each plate bearing the name of the person who is to occupy the place. Plain cards are well enough; but the French design (they are designed in this country also) beautiful cards for the purpose, illustrated with varieties of devices: some are rollicking cherubs with capricious antics, who present different tempting viands; autumn leaves and delicate flowers in chromo form pretty surroundings for the names on others; yet the designs are so various on these and the bill-of-fare cards that each hostess may seek to find new ones, while frequent dinner-goers may have interesting collections of these mementoes, which may serve to recall the occasions in after-years.

6th. If the dinner is intended to be particularly fine, have bills of fare, one for each person, written on little sheets of paper smoothly cut in half, or on French bill-of-fare cards, which come for the purpose. If expense is no object, and you entertain enough to justify it, have cards for your own use especially engraved. Have your crest, or perhaps a monogram, at the top of the card, and forms for different courses following, so headed that you have only to fill out the space with the special dishes for the occasion. I will give the example of a form. The forms are often seen on the dinner-cards; yet, perhaps, they are as often omitted, when the bills of fare are written, like those given at the end of the book.

Bills of fare are generally written in French. It is a pity that our own rich language is inadequate to the duties of a fashionable bill of fare, especially when, perhaps, all the guests do not understand the Gallic tongue, and the bill of fare (*menu*) for their accommodation might as well be written in Choctaw. I will arrange a table with French names of dishes for the aid of those preferring the French bills of fare. I would say that some tact might be displayed in choosing which language to employ.

MENU.

———

Dîner du 15 Février.

———

Potages.
Poissons.
Hors-d'œuvres.
Relevés.
Entrées.
Rôtis.
Entremêts.
Glaces.
Dessert.

If you are entertaining a ceremonious company, with tastes for the frivolities of the world, or, perhaps, foreign embassadors, use unhesitatingly the French bills of fare; but practical uncles and substantial persons of learning and wit, who, perhaps, do not appreciate the merits of languages which they do not understand, might consider you demented to place one of these effusions before them. I would advise the English bills of fare on these occasions.

7th. The attendants at table should make no noise. They should wear slippers or light boots. "Nothing so distinguishes the style of perfectly appointed houses from vulgar imitations as the quiet, self-possessed movements of the attendants." No word should be spoken among them during dinner, nor should they even seem to notice the conversation of the company at table.

8th. The waiter should wear a dress-coat, white vest, black trousers, and white necktie; the waiting-maid, a neat black alpaca or a clean calico dress, with a white apron.

9th. Although I would advise these rules to be generally followed, yet it is as pleasant a change to see an individuality or a characteristic taste displayed in the setting of the table and the choice of dishes as in the appointments of our houses or in matters of toilet. At different seasons the table might be changed to wear a more appropriate garb. It may be solid, rich, and showy, or simple, light, and fresh.

10th. Aim to have a variety or change in dishes. It is as necessary to the stomach and to the enjoyment of the table as is change of scene for the mind. Even large and expensive state dinners become very monotonous when one finds everywhere the same choice of dishes. Mr. Walker, in his "Original," says: "To order dinner is a matter of invention and combination. It involves novelty, simplicity, and taste; whereas, in the generality of dinners, there is no character but that of routine, according to the season."

11th. Although many fashionable dinners are of from three to four hours' duration, I think every minute over two hours is a "stately durance vile." After that time, one can have no appetite; conversation must be forced. It is preferable to have the dinner a short one than a minute too long. If one rises from a fine dinner wearied and satiated, the memory of the whole occasion must be tinged with this last impression.

12th. There is a variety of opinions as to who should be first served at table. Many of the *haut monde* insist that the hostess should be first attended to. Once, when visiting a family with an elegant establishment, who, with cultivated tastes and years of traveling experience, prided themselves on their *savoir faire*, one of the members said, "Yes, if Queen Victoria were our guest, our sister, who presides at table, should always be served first." The custom originated in ancient times, when the hospitable fashion of poisoning was in vogue. Then the guests preferred to see the hostess partake of each dish before venturing themselves. Poisoning is not now the order of the day, beyond what is accomplished by rich pastry and plum-puddings. If there be but one attendant, the lady guest sitting at the right of the host or the oldest lady should be first served. There are certain natural instincts of propriety which fashion or custom can not regulate. As soon as the second person is helped, there should be no further waiting before eating.

13th. Have chairs of equal height at table. Perhaps every one may know by experience the trial to his good humor in finding himself perched above or sunk below the general level.

14th. The selection of china for the table offers an elegant field in which to display one's taste. The most economical choice for durability is this: put your extra money in a handsome dessert set, all (except the plates) of which are displayed on the table all the time during dinner; then select the remainder of the service in plain white, or white and gilt, china. When any dish is broken, it can be easily matched and replaced.

A set of china decorated in color to match the color of the dining-room is exceedingly tasteful. This choice is not an economical one, as it is necessary to replace broken pieces by having new ones manufactured—an expense quite equal to the extra trouble required to imitate a dish made in another country.

By far the most elegant arrangement consists in having different sets of plates, each set of a different pattern, for every course. Here is an unlimited field for exquisite taste. Let the meat and vegetable dishes be of plated silver. Let the *épergne* or centre-piece (holding flowers or fruit) be of silver, or perhaps it might be preferred of majolica, of bisque, or of glass. The majolica ware is very fashionable now, and dessert, oyster, and salad sets of it are exceedingly pretty. A set of majolica plates, imitating pink shells, with a large pink-shell platter, is very pretty, and appropriate for almost any course. Oyster-plates in French ware imitate five oyster-shells, with a miniature cup in the centre for holding the lemon. There are other patterns of oyster-plates in majolica of the most gorgeous colors, where each rim is concaved in six shells to hold as many oysters. The harlequin dessert sets are interesting, where every plate is not only different in design and color, but is a specimen of different kinds of ware as well. In these sets the Dresden, French, and painted plates of any ware that suits the fancy are combined.

A set of plates for a course at dinner is unique in the Chinese or Japanese patterns. Dessert sets of Bohemian glass or of cut-glass are a novelty; however, the painted sets seem more appropriate for the dessert (fruits, etc.), while glass sets are tasteful for jellies, cold puddings, etc., or what are called the cold *entremêts* served just before the dessert proper.

But it seems difficult, in entering the Colamores' and other large places of the kind in New York, to know what to select, there are such myriads of exquisite plates, table ornaments, and fairy-lands of glass.

I consider the table ornaments in silver much less attractive than those in fancy ware. There are lovely maidens in bisque, reclining, while they hold painted oval dishes for a jelly, a Bavarian cream, or for flowers or fruit; cherub boys in majolica, tugging away with wheelbarrows, which should be loaded with flowers; antique water-jugs; cheese-plates in Venetian glass; clusters of lilies from mirror bases to hold flowers or *bonbons*; tripods of dolphins, with great pink mouths, to hold salt and pepper.

If a lady, with tastes to cultivate in her family, can afford elegancies in dress, let her retrench in that, and bid farewell to all her ugly and insipid white china; let wedding presents consist more of these ornaments (which may serve to decorate any room), and less of silver salt-cellars, pepper-stands, and pickle-forks.

Senator Sumner was a lover of the ceramic art. His table presented a delightful study to the connoisseur, with its different courses of plates, all different and *recherché* in design. Nothing aroused this inimitable host at a dinner party from his literary labors more effectually than a special announcement to him by Marley of the arrival from Europe of a new set of quaint and elegant specimens of China ware. He would repair to New York on the next train.

15th. I will close these suggestions by copying from an English book a practical drill exercise for serving at table. The dishes are served from the side-table.

"Let us suppose a table laid for eight persons, dressed in its best; as attendants, only two persons—a butler and a footman, or one of these, with a page or neat waiting-maid; and let us suppose some one stationed outside the door in the butler's pantry to do nothing but fetch up, or hand, or carry off dishes, one by one:

While guests are being seated, person from outside brings up soup;
Footman receives soup at door;
Butler serves it out;
Footman hands it;
Both change plates.
Footman takes out soup, and receives fish at door; while butler hands wine;
Butler serves out fish;
Footman hands it (plate in one hand, and sauce in the other);
Both change plates.
Footman brings in *entrée*, while butler hands wine;
Butler hands *entrée*;
Footman hands vegetables;
Both change plates,
Etc., etc.

"The carving of the joint seems the only difficulty. However, it will not take long for an expert carver to cut eight pieces."

THE DINNER PARTY.

It is very essential, in giving a dinner party, to know precisely how many guests one is to entertain. It is a serious inconvenience to have any doubt on this subject. Consequently, it is well to send an invitation, which may be in the following form:

> *Mrs. Smith requests the pleasure of Mr. Jones's company at dinner, on Thursday, January 5th, at seven o'clock.*
>
> R. S. V. P.
>
> *12 New York Avenue, January 2d, 1875.*

The capital letters constitute the initials of four French words, meaning, "Answer, if you please" (*Répondez s'il vous plait*). The person thus invited must not fail to reply at once, sending a messenger to the door with the note. It is considered impolite to send it by post.

If the person invited has any doubt about being able to attend the dinner at the time stated, he should decline the invitation at once. He should be positive one way or the other, not delaying the question for consideration more than a day at the utmost. If Mr. Jones should then decline, he might reply as follows:

> *Mr. Jones regrets that he is unable to accept Mrs. Smith's polite invitation for Thursday evening.*
>
> *8 Thirty-seventh Street, January 3d.*

Or,

> *Mr. Jones regrets that a previous engagement prevents his acceptance of Mrs. Smith's polite invitation for Thursday evening.*
> Thirty-seventh Street, January 3d.

A prompt and decided answer of this character enables Mrs. Smith to supply the place with some other person, thereby preventing that most disagreeable thing, a vacant chair at table.

If the invitation be accepted, Mr. Jones might say in his note:

> *Mr. Jones accepts, with pleasure, Mrs. Smith's invitation for Thursday evening.*
> Thirty-seventh Street, January 2d.

The more simple the invitation or reply, the better. Do not attempt any high-flown or original modes. Originality is most charming on most occasions; this is not one of them.

In New York, many, I notice, seem to think it elegant to use the French construction of sentences in formal notes: for instance, they are particular to say, "the invitation of Mrs. Smith," instead of "Mrs. Smith's invitation;" and "2d January," instead of "January 2d." In writing in the French language, the French construction of sentences would seem eminently proper. One might be pardoned for laughing at an English construction, if ignorance were not the cause. So, when one writes in English, let the sentences be concise, and according to the rules of the language.

On the appointed day, the guest should endeavor to arrive at the house not exceeding ten minutes before the time fixed for dinner; and while he avoids a too early arrival, he should be equally careful about being tardy.

It is enough to disturb the serenity and good temper of the most amiable hostess during the whole evening for a guest to delay her dinner, impairing it, of course, to a great extent. She should not be expected to wait over fifteen minutes for any one. Perhaps it would be as well for her to order dinner ten minutes after the appointed hour in her invitation, to meet the possible contingency of delay on the part of some guest.

When the guests are assembled in the drawing-room, if the company be large, the host or hostess can quietly intimate to the gentlemen what ladies they will respectively accompany to the dining-room. After a few moments of conversation and introductions, the dinner is to be announced, when the host should offer his arm to the lady guest of honor, the hostess taking the arm of the gentleman guest of honor; and now, the host leading the way, all should follow; the hostess, with her escort, being the last to leave the drawing-room. They should find their places at table with as little confusion as possible, not sitting down until the hostess is seated. After dinner is over, the hostess giving the signal by moving back her chair, all should leave the dining-room. The host may then invite the gentlemen to the smoking-room or library. The ladies should repair to the drawing-room. A short time thereafter (perhaps in half an hour), the butler should bring to the drawing-room the tea-service on a salver, with a cake-basket filled with fancy biscuits, or rather crackers or little cakes.

Placing them on the table, he may then announce to the host that tea is served. The gentlemen join the ladies; and, after a chat of a few minutes over the tea, all of the guests may take their departure. If the attendant is a waiting-maid, and the tea-service rather heavy, she might bring two or three cups filled with tea, and a small sugar-bowl and cream-pitcher, also the cake-basket, on a small salver; and when the cups are passed, return for more.

I do not like the English fashion, which requires the ladies to retire from the table, leaving the gentlemen to drink more wine, and smoke. Enough wine is drunk during dinner. English customs are admirable, generally, and one naturally inclines to adopt them; but in this instance I do not hesitate to condemn and reject a custom in which I see no good, but, on the contrary, a temptation to positive evil. The French reject it; let Americans do the same.

COOKING AS AN ACCOMPLISHMENT.

THE reason why cooking in America is, as a rule, so inferior is not because American women are less able and apt than the women of France, and not because the American men do not discuss and appreciate the merits of good cooking and the pleasure of entertaining friends at their own table; it is merely because American women seem possessed with the idea that it is not the fashion to know how to cook; that, as an accomplishment, the art of cooking is not as ornamental as that of needle-work or piano-playing. I do not undervalue these last accomplishments. A young lady of *esprit* should understand them; but she should understand, also, the accomplishment of cooking. A young lady can scarcely have too many accomplishments, for they serve to adorn her home, and are attractive and charming, generally. But of them all—painting, music, fancy work, or foreign language—is there one more fascinating and useful, or one which argues more intelligence in its acquisition, than the accomplishment of cooking?

What would more delight Adolphus than to discover that his pretty *fiancée*, Julia, was an accomplished cook; that with her dainty fingers she could gracefully dash off a creamy omelet, and by miraculous manœuvres could produce to his astonished view a dozen different kaleidoscopic omelets, *aux fines herbes, aux huîtres, aux petits pois, aux tomates*, etc.; and not only that, but scientific croquettes, mysterious soups, delicious salads, marvelous sauces, and the hundred and one savory results of a little artistic skill? Delighted Adolphus—if a sensible man, and such a woman should have no other than a sensible man—would consider this as the *chef-d'œuvre* of all her accomplishments, as he regarded her the charming assurance of so many future comforts.

From innate coquetry alone the French women appreciate the powers of their dainty table. Cooking is an art they cultivate. Any of the *haut monde* are proud to originate a new dish, many famous ones doing them credit in bearing their names.

One thing is quite evident in America—that the want of this ornamental and useful information is most deplorable. The inefficiency, in this respect, of Western and Southern women, brought up under the system of slavery, is somewhat greater than that of the women of the Northern and Eastern States; however, as a nation, there is little to praise in this regard in any locality. Professor Blot endeavored to come to the rescue. Every *man* applauded his enterprise; yet I can myself testify to the indifference of the women—his classes for the study of cookery numbering by units where they should have numbered by hundreds. He soon discontinued his instructive endeavors, and at last died a poor man.

There is little difficulty abroad in obtaining good cooks at reasonable prices, who have pursued regular courses of instruction in their trade: not so in America. Hospitality demands the entertaining of friends at the social board; yet it is almost impossible to do so in this country in an acceptable manner, unless the hostess herself not only has a proper idea of the serving of a table, but of the art of cooking the dishes themselves as well. In some of the larger cities, satisfactory dinners and trained waiters may be provided at an enormous cost at the famous restaurants, where the meal may appear home-like and elegant. But unfortunate is the woman, generally, who wants to do "the correct thing," and, wishing to entertain at dinner, relies upon the sense, good taste, and management of the proprietor of a restaurant. She may confidently rely upon one thing—an extortionate bill; and, generally, as well, upon a vulgar display, which poorly imitates the manner of refined private establishments.

However, "living for the world" seems very contemptible in comparison with the importance of that wholesome, satisfactory, every-day living which so vitally concerns the health and pleasure of the family circle.

But why waste time in asserting these self-evident facts? They are acknowledged and proclaimed every day by suffering humanity; yet the difficulty is not remedied. Is there a remedy, then? Yes. This is a free country, yet Dame Fashion is the Queen. Make it the fashion, then, that the art and science of cookery shall be classed among the necessary accomplishments of every well-educated lady. This is a manifest duty on the part of ladies of influence and position, even if the object be only for the benefit of the country at large. Let these ladies be accomplished artists in cookery. The rest will soon follow. There will be plenty of imitators.

Many ladies of rank in England have written valuable books on cookery, and on the effects resulting from the want of the knowledge. None wrote better than Lady Morgan. Speaking of clubs, she says:

"The social want of the times, however, brought its remedy along with it, and the reaction was astounding.... Then it was that clubs arose—homes of refuge to destitute celibacy, chapels of ease to discontented husbands. There, men could dine, like gentlemen and Christians, upon all the *friandises* of the French kitchen, much cheaper and far more wholesomely than at their own tables upon the tough, half-sodden fibres of the national roast and boiled, or on the hazardous resources of hash, gravy soup, and marrow puddings.

"Moral England gave in. The English 'home'—that temple of the heart, that centre of all the virtues—was left to the solitary enjoyment of the English wives.

"To your *casseroles*, then, women of Britain! Would you, with a falconer's voice, lure your faithless tassels back again? Apply to the practical remedy of your wrongs; proceed to the reform of your domestic government, and turn your thoughts to that art which, coming into action every day in the year during the longest life, includes within its circles the whole philosophy of economy and order, the preservation of good health, and the tone of good society—and all peculiarly within your province."

BREAKFAST.

AFTER a fast of twelve or thirteen hours, the system requires something substantial as preparation for the labors of the day; consequently, I consider the American breakfasts more desirable for an active people than those of France or England.

In France, the first breakfast consists merely of a cup of coffee and a roll. A second breakfast, at eleven o'clock, is more substantial, dishes being served which may be eaten with a fork (*déjeuner à la fourchette*), as a chop with a potato *soufflé*. No wonder there are *cafés* in Paris where American breakfasts are advertised, for it takes one of our nationality a very short time to become dissatisfied with this meagre first meal.

In England, breakfast is a very informal meal. After some fatiguing occasion, if one should desire the luxury of an extra nap, he is not mercilessly expected at the table simply because it is the breakfast-hour; for there the breakfast-hour is any time one chances to be ready for it. Gentlemen and ladies read their papers and letters in the breakfast-room—a practice which, of course, is more agreeable for guests than convenient for servants. However, if one can afford it, why not? This habit requires a little different setting of the table. It is decorated with flowers or plants, and upon it are placed several kinds of breads, fruits, melons, potted meats, and freshest of boiled eggs. But the substantial dishes must be served from the sideboard, where they are kept in silver chafing-dishes over spirit-lamps. As members of the family or guests enter, the servant helps them each once, then leaves the room. If they have further wants, they help themselves or ring a bell.

The American breakfast is all placed upon the table, unless oatmeal porridge should be served as a first course. Changes of plates are also necessary when cakes requiring sirup or when melons or fruits are served.

Let us now set the American breakfast-table.

The coffee-urn and silver service necessary are placed in a straight line before the hostess. The one or two kinds of substantials are set before the host; vegetables or *entrées* are placed on the sides. Do not have them askew. It is quite as easy for an attendant to place a dish in a straight line as in an oblique angle with every other dish on the table.

I advocate the general use of oatmeal porridge for breakfast. Nothing is more wholesome, and nothing more relished after a little use. If not natural, the taste should be acquired. It is invaluable for children, and of no less benefit for persons of mature years. Nearly all the little Scotch and Irish children are brought up on it. When Queen Victoria first visited Scotland, she noticed the particularly ruddy and healthy appearance of the children, and, after inquiry about their diet and habits, became at once a great advocate for the use of porridge. She used it for her own children, and it was at once introduced very generally into England. Another of its advantages is that serving it as a first course enables the cook to prepare many dishes, such as steaks, omelets, etc., just as the family sit down to breakfast; and when the porridge is eaten, she is ready with the other dishes "smoking hot."

It would be well if more attention were given to breakfasts than is usually bestowed. The table might have a fresher look with flowers or a flowering plant in the centre. The breakfast napery is very pretty now, with colored borders to suit the color of the room, the table-cloth and napkins matching.

The beefsteaks should be varied, for instance, one morning with a tomato sauce, another *à la maître d'hôtel*, or with a brown sauce, or garnished with water-cresses, green pease, fried potatoes, potato-balls, etc., instead of being always the same beefsteak, too frequently overcooked or undercooked, and often floating in butter.

Melons, oranges, compotes, any and all kinds of fruits, should be served at breakfast. In the season, sliced tomatoes, with a French or *Mayonnaise* dressing, is a most refreshing breakfast dish. A great resource is in the variety of omelets, and with a little practice, nothing is so easily made. One morning it may be a plain omelet; another, with macaroni and cheese; another, with fine herbs; another, with little strips of ham or with oysters. The English receipt on page 148 makes a pleasant change for a veal cutlet. When chickens are no longer very young, the receipt on page 175 (deviled chicken), with a Cunard sauce or a white sauce, is another change. The different arrangements of meat-balls and croquettes, with tomato, cream, apple, or brown sauces, are delicious when they are freshly and carefully made.

As there are hundreds of delicious breakfast dishes, which only require a little attention and interest to understand, how unfortunate it must be for a man to have a wife who has nothing for breakfast but an alternation of juiceless beefsteak, greasy and ragged mutton-chops, and swimming hash, with unwholesome hot breads to make up deficiencies!

Breakfast parties are very fashionable, being less expensive than dinners, and just as satisfactory to guests. They are served generally about ten o'clock, although any time from ten to twelve o'clock may be chosen for the purpose. It seems to me that ten o'clock, or even nine o'clock (it depends upon the persons invited), is the preferable hour. Guests might prefer to retain their strength by a repast at home if the breakfast-hour were at twelve o'clock, and then the fine breakfast would be less appreciated. At breakfast parties, with the exception of the silver service being on the table all the time for tea and coffee, the dishes are served in courses precisely as for dinner.

In England, breakfast parties are perhaps more in favor than lunch parties, especially among the *literati*. Macaulay said, when extolling the merits of breakfast parties as compared with all other entertainments, "Dinner parties are mere formalities; but you invite a man to breakfast because you want to see *him*."

Three bills of fare are given for breakfast parties, which will show the order of different courses:

Winter Breakfast.

1st Course.—Broiled sardines on toast, garnished with slices of lemon. Tea, coffee, or chocolate.

2d Course.—Larded sweet-breads, garnished with French pease. Cold French rolls or petits pains. Sauterne.

3d Course.—Small fillets or the tender cuts from porter-house-steaks, served on little square slices of toast, with mushrooms.

4th Course.—Fried oysters; breakfast puffs.

5th Course.—Fillets of grouse (each fillet cut in two), on little thin slices of fried mush, garnished with potatoes à la Parisienne.

6th Course.—Sliced oranges, with sugar.

7th Course.—Waffles, with maple sirup.

Early Spring Breakfast.

1st Course.—An Havana orange for each person, dressed on a fork (page 338).

2d Course.—Boiled shad, maître d'hôtel sauce; Saratoga potatoes. Tea or coffee.

3d Course.—Lamb-chops, tomato sauce. Château Yquem.

4th Course.—Omelet, with green pease, or garnished with parsley and thin diamonds of ham, or with shrimps, etc., etc.

5th Course.—Fillets of beef, garnished with water-cresses and little round radishes; muffins.

6th Course.—Rice pancakes, with maple sirup.

Summer Breakfast.

1st Course.—Melons.

2d Course.—Little fried perch, smelts, or trout, with a sauce Tartare, the dish garnished with shrimps and olives. Coffee, tea, or chocolate.

3d Course.—Young chickens, sautéd, with cream-gravy, surrounded with potatoes à la neige. Claret.

4th Course.—Poached eggs on anchovy-toast.

5th Course.—Little fillets of porter-house-steaks, with tomatoes à la Mayonnaise.

6th Course.—Peaches, quartered, sweetened, and half-frozen.

LUNCH.

This is more especially a ladies' meal. If one gives a lunch party, ladies alone are generally invited. It is an informal meal on ordinary occasions, when every thing is placed upon the table at once. A servant remains in the room only long enough to serve the first round of dishes, then leaves, supposing that confidential conversation may be desired. Familiar friends often "happen in" to lunch, and are always to be expected.

Some fashionable ladies have the reputation of having very fine lunches—chops, chickens, oysters, salads, chocolate, and many other good things being provided; and others, just as fashionable, have nothing but a cup of tea or chocolate, some thin slices of bread and butter, and cold meat; or, if of Teutonic taste, nothing but cheese, crackers, and ale, thus reserving the appetite for dinner.

In entertaining at lunch, the dishes are served in the same manner as for dinner. Each dish is served as a separate course. It may be placed on the table before the hostess, if the lunch party is not very large; but it is generally served from the side. The table is also decorated in the same manner as for dinner, with a centre-piece of flowers or of fruit, and with various *compotiers* around the centre, containing fruits, *bonbons*, little fancy cakes, Indian or other preserves, etc. Other ornaments, in Dresden china, majolica ware, Venetian or French glass, etc., filled with flowers, are often seen. Little dishes of common glass in different shapes, as crosses, quarter-moons, etc., about an inch high (see cuts, page 58), are also filled with flowers, and placed at symmetrical distances. As the last-mentioned decorations are very cheap, every one may indulge in them, and consider that there are no more beautiful ornaments, after all.

The lunch-table is generally covered with a colored table-cloth.

The principal dishes served are *patés*, croquettes, shell-fish, game, salads—in fact, all kinds of *entrées* and cold desserts, or I may say dishes are preferred which do not require carving. *Bouillon* is generally served as a first course in *bouillon* cups, which are quite like large coffee-cups, or coffee or tea cups may be used, although any dinner soup served in soup-plates is *en regle*. A cup of chocolate, with whipped cream on the top, is often served as another course.

I will give five bills of fare, reserved from five very nice little lunch parties:

Mrs. Collier's Lunch (February 2d).
Bouillon; sherry.
Roast oysters on half-shell; Sauterne.
Little vols-au-vent of oysters.
Thin scollops, or cuts of fillet of beef, braised; French pease; Champagne.
Chicken croquettes, garnished with fried parsley; potato croquettes.
Cups of chocolate, with whipped cream.
Salad—lettuce dressed with tarragon.
Biscuits glacés; fruit-ices.
Fruit.
Bonbons.

Mrs. Sprague's Lunch (March 10th).
Raw oysters on half-shell.
Bouillon; sherry.
Little vols-au-vent of sweet-breads.
Lamb-chops; tomato sauce; Champagne.
Chicken croquettes; French pease.
Snipe; potatoes à la Parisienne.
Salad of lettuce.
Neuchâtel cheese; milk wafers, toasted.
Chocolate Bavarian cream, molded in little cups, with a spoonful of peach marmalade on each plate.
Vanilla ice-cream; fancy cakes.
Fruit.

Mrs. Miller's Lunch (January 6th).
Bouillon.
Deviled crabs; olives; claret punch.
Sweet-breads à la Milanaise.
Fillets of grouse, currant jelly; Saratoga potatoes.
Roman punch.
Fried oysters, garnished with chow-chow.
Chicken salad, or, rather, Mayonnaise of chicken.

Ramikins.
Wine jelly, and whipped cream.
Napolitaine ice-cream.
Fruit.
Bonbons.

Mrs. Wells's Lunch.
Bouillon; sherry.
Fried frogs' legs; French pease.
Smelts, sauce Tartare; potatoes à la Parisienne.
Chicken in scallop-shells; Champagne.
Sweet-bread croquettes; tomato sauce.
Fried cream.
Salad; Romaine.
Welsh rare-bit.
Peaches and cream, frozen; fancy cakes.
Fruits.

Mrs. Filley's Lunch.
Mock-turtle soup; English milk-punch.
Lobster-chops; claret.
Mushrooms in crust.
Lamb-chops, en papillote.
Chetney of slices of baked fillet of beef.
Chocolate, with whipped cream.
Spinach on tongue slices (page 145), sauce Tartare.
Roast quail, bread sauce (page 185).
Cheese; lettuce, garnished with slices of radishes and nasturtium blossoms,
French dressing.
Mince-meat patties; Champagne.
Ices and fancy cakes.
Fruit.

GENTLEMEN'S SUPPERS.

As ladies have exclusive lunches, gentlemen have exclusive suppers. Nearly the same dishes are served for suppers as for lunches, although gentlemen generally prefer more game and wine. Sometimes they like fish suppers, with two or three or more varieties of fish, when nightmare might be written at the end of the bill of fare.

If one has not a reliable cook, it is very convenient to give these entertainments, as the hostess has a chance to station herself in the *cuisine*, and personally superintend the supper.

One bill of fare is given for a fish supper:

1st Course.—Raw oysters served in a block of ice (page 113). [The ice has a pretty effect in the gas-light.]
2d Course.—Shad, maître d'hôtel sauce, garnished with smelts.
3d Course.—Sweet-breads and tomato sauce.
4th Course.—Boiled sardines, on toast.
5th Course.—Deviled chicken, Cunard sauce.
6th Course.—Fillets of duck, with salad of lettuce.
7th Course.—Mayonnaise of salmon, garnished with shrimps.
8th Course.—Welsh rare-bit.
9th Course.—Charlotte Russe.
10th Course.—Ice-cream and cake.

EVENING PARTIES.

If people can afford to give large evening parties, it is less trouble and more satisfactory to place the supper in the hands of the confectioner.

For card parties or small companies of thirty or forty persons, to meet some particular stranger, or for literary reunions, the trouble need not be great. People would entertain more if the trouble were less.

If one has a regular reception-evening, ices, cake, and chocolate are quite enough; or for chocolate might be substituted sherry or a bowl of punch.

For especial occasions for a company of thirty or forty, a table prettily set with some flowers, fruit, chicken salad, croquettes or sweet-breads and pease, one or two or more kinds of ice-cream and cakes, is quite sufficient. Either coffee and tea, Champagne, a bowl of punch or of eggnog, would be sufficient in the way of beverage.

SOMETHING ABOUT ECONOMY.

I am indebted to a French girl living in our family for the substance of this chapter. Her parents being obliged to live in a most economical way in St. Louis, still had an uncommonly good table. One resource was a little garden, in which small compass were raised enough onions, tomatoes, carrots, and a few other vegetables, to nearly supply the family. A small bed of four feet square, surrounded by a pretty border of lettuce, was large enough for raising all necessary herbs, such as sage, summer savory, thyme, etc. Little boxes in the kitchen windows contained growing parsley, ever ready for use.

I give receipts for three of their soups—the onion, vegetable *purée*, and potato soups being most excellent, and costing not over from five to ten cents each. One of their dinner dishes was a heart (10 cents) stuffed, baked two or three hours, and served with a brown gravy and an onion garnish (see receipt). Still another was a two-pound round-steak (20 cents), spread with a bread and sage stuffing, then rolled, tied, floured, seasoned on top, then baked, basting it often. It was a pretty dish, with tomato sauce around it. Sometimes a cheap fish was cut in slices, egged and bread-crumbed, fried, and garnished with fried potatoes. They had always a salad for dinner, prepared from their border of lettuce, some cold potatoes, cold beans, or other vegetable. A fine breakfast dish was of kidneys (5 cents). Few Americans know how to cook kidneys, and butchers often throw them away; yet in France they are considered a great delicacy.

Their *répertoire* of cheap dishes was large; so there was always a change for, at least, each day of the week. A crumb of bread was never wasted. All odd morsels were dried in the oven, pounded, and put away in a tin-box, ready for breading cutlets cut from any pieces of mutton or veal, and for many other purposes.

Any pieces of suet or drippings were clarified and put one side, to be used for frying. Remains of cooked vegetables of any kind were saved for soups and sauces. Not a slice of a tomato nor leaf of a cabbage was thrown away.

If they had butter that was not entirely sweet, they added more salt, a little soda, brought it to a boil on the stove, and then put it away in a little crock. By allowing the settlings to remain at the bottom, the butter became entirely sweet, and not too salt for cooking purposes.

Chickens, cutlets, etc., were larded at this table. Now, just to mention the word "larding" is to overwhelm a common cook; and to require it, is to rivet in the minds of most housewives the entire impracticability of a whole receipt in which it is an item. Pieces of salt pork or breakfast bacon should always be kept in the house. A pound of it, which is not expensive, may last a long time, as it requires very little for flavoring many things; then, if one has any idea of sewing, or what it is to push a needle through any thing, one can lard. It only requires a larding-needle, which costs fifteen cents, and which should last a century. By placing little cut strips of pork in the end of the needle, as is explained among "directions," then drawing the needle through parts of the meat, leaving the pork midway, this wonderfully difficult operation is accomplished. It is only a few minutes' pastime to lard turkeys, chickens, birds, cutlets, sweet-breads, etc., which gives to them flavor and style.

Limited in fortune as were this family, they were never without stock at hand. Their meat for croquettes, patties, etc., had served a duty to the soup-kettle. If a chicken was to be boiled for the table, it was thrown into the stock-pot while the soup was simmering, and thus it and the chicken were both benefited.

Their meat dishes were often garnished with little potato-balls, cooked *à la Parisienne*, or simply boiled. This seemed extravagant; but as a French vegetable-cutter only costs twenty-five cents, and the balls can be cut very rapidly—all the parings boiled and mashed serving another time as potato-cakes—there was nothing wasted, and little time lost.

In short, this household (and it is a sample of nearly all French families of limited means) lived well on little more than many an American family would throw away.

Let me give five bills of fare of their dinners, the second of which is partly prepared from the remains of the first day:

Beef soup (soup bone), 10 cents.
Veal blanquette and boiled potatoes (knuckle of veal), 15 cents.
Salad of sliced tomatoes, 2 or 3 cents.
Boiled rice, with a border of stewed small pears (green, or of common

variety), 10 cents.
Onion or bean soup, 5 cents.
Fish (en matelote), 15 cents.
Croquettes (made of the remains of the cold beef-soup meat, and rice), with a tomato sauce.
Salad of cold boiled potatoes.
Fried bread-pudding.

———

Potato soup.
Round steak, rolled (page 140), with baked, parboiled onions, 25 cents.
Salad of lettuce.
Apple-fritters, with sirup.

———

Tomato soup.
Beef à la mode, with spinach, 40 cents (enough for two dinners).
Salad of potatoes and parsley.
Rice-pudding.

———

Noodle soup.
Mutton ragout, with potatoes, 25 cents.
Noodles and stuffed tomatoes.
Cheese omelet.

———

DIRECTIONS AND EXPLANATIONS.

Boiling.

Fowls or joints should be tied or well skewered into shape before boiling.

Every thing should be *gently* simmered, rather than fast boiled, in order to be tender. The water should never be allowed to stop simmering before the article is quite done. A pudding is thus entirely ruined.

The kettle should be kept covered, merely raising the cover at times to remove the scum. Boiled fowl, with a white sauce, is a favorite English dish, and very nice it is if properly prepared.

Frying.

Frying means cooking by *immersion* in hot fat, butter, or oil. There is no English word for what is called frying in a spoonful of fat, first on one side, and then on the other. *Sauté* is the French word, and should be Anglicized. Ordinary cooks, instead of frying, invariably *sauté* every thing. Almost every article that is usually *sautéd* is much better and more economical *fried*; as, for instance, oysters, fish, birds, cutlets, crabs, etc.

The fat should always be tested before the article is immersed. A little piece of bread may be thrown in, and if it colors quickly, the fat is ready, and not before. The temperature of hot grease, it will be remembered, is much greater than that of boiling water, which can not exceed a certain degree of heat, whether it boil slow or fast. Hot grease reaches a very high degree of heat, and consequently the surface of any thing is almost instantaneously hardened or crisped when thrown into it. The inside is thus kept free from grease, and is quickly cooked. An article first dipped in egg and bread-crumbs should be *entirely* free from grease when thus cooked, as the egg is hardened the instant it touches the hot grease, and the oyster, croquette, cutlet, or sweet-bread is perfectly protected. The same fat can be used repeatedly for frying the same thing. The fat in which fish is fried should not be again used for any thing except fish. Professional cooks have several frying-kettles, in which fat is kept for frying different things. A little kettle for frying potatoes exclusively should always be at hand.

One will see that this style of cooking is economical, as there is very little waste of fat; and then fried articles need no other dressing.

After frying fish, meat, or vegetables, let the fat stand about five minutes; strain, and then return it to the kettle, which should always be kept covered, after it is once cold.

Beef suet, salted, is quite as good for frying as lard, and is much cheaper. It is well to purchase it by the pound, and have it rendered in the kitchen.

To Prepare Grease for Frying (*Professor Blot*).

Take beef suet, the part around the kidneys, or any kind of fat, raw or cooked, and free of fibres, nerves, thin skin, or bones; chop it fine; add to it whatever you may have of fat skimmed off the top of meat soup; put it in a cast-iron or crockery kettle; set it on a moderate fire; boil gently for fifteen minutes; skim it well during the process; take from the fire, leave it five minutes, and then strain it; after which, put it in pots, and keep them in a dry and cool place; cover the pots well every time you have occasion to use, but never cover them while the grease is warm. This grease is as good, if not better than any other to fry fish, fritters, and other similar things, which require to be entirely covered with grease.[A]

Broiling.

I did not appreciate the nicety of broiling until, upon an occasion, a gentleman invited a dinner company to a private dining-room of one of our large restaurants, to eat a certain kind of fish, which he considered especially fine. The host was quite out of humor to see the fish come to the table baked, when he had ordered it broiled. The proprietor afterward explained that, for some reason, his French cook was absent for that day, and he had no other who could broil so large a fish. I at once realized that, after all, it must be a delicate and difficult thing to broil a large fish, so that the centre would be well done, and the surface not burned. The smaller and thinner the article, the hotter should be the fire; the larger the article, the more temperate the fire, or, rather, the greater distance it should at first be placed from it. The fish, in this case, should have been wrapped in oiled or buttered paper. It should have been placed rather near the fire for the first few moments; then removed farther away, or placed on another more moderate fire. A large baking-pan should have covered the top of the fish, to hold the heat. When nearly done, the paper should have been removed, to allow the surface to brown.

Always grease the gridiron well, and have it *hot*, before the meat is placed on it. Any thing egged and bread-crumbed should be buttered before it is broiled. Fish should be buttered and sprinkled with flour, which will prevent the skin from adhering to the gridiron. Cutlets, and in fact every thing, are more delicate buttered before broiling. A little lemon-juice is also often a nice addition. Birds, and other things which need to be halved, should be broiled, *inside* first.

Remember that a hot, clear fire is necessary for cooking all small articles. They should be turned often, to be cooked evenly, without being burned.

Never put a fork in the lean part of meat on the gridiron, as it allows the juice to escape.

Always cover the gridiron with a tin pan or a baking-pan. The sooner the meat is cooked without burning, the better. The pan holds the heat, and often prevents a stray line of smoke from touching the meat.

If the fire should be too hot, sprinkle salt over it.

Roasting.

There is little use to talk about roasting, as but few will attempt it, always considering it easier to bake instead. Indeed, there is so little demand in many sections for stoves and ranges suited to the purpose that they are difficult to obtain. Of course, there is no comparison between these modes of cooking. Beef, mutton, turkeys, ducks, or birds—in fact, any kind of meat is tenfold better roasted than baked. In Europe, all these articles are roasted; and people there would have great contempt for a piece of beef or a turkey baked. In New York and Philadelphia, also, at the finer establishments, the meats are generally roasted. The trouble is little greater than to bake. It is only necessary to have the range or stove constructed for roasting, and a tin screen, with a spit and jack, to place before the coals. Some of the roasters are arranged with a spring-jack. The meat is placed on the spit, and the spring wound up, which sets the meat to revolving slowly before the fire.

In roasting, the meat should at first be placed near the coals, so as to quickly harden the surface; then it should be removed back a little distance, to be cooked through, without burning. The oftener it is basted, the better it is. If the roast of meat is very large, it should be surrounded with a buttered paper.

Just before the meat is done, it should be basted with a little butter or drippings, then sprinkled with flour, and placed nearer the fire, to brown nicely, when it will take a frothy appearance.

Much depends upon the management of the fire. It should be made some time before the meat is placed for roasting, so that the coals may be bright and hot. It should also be strong enough to last, with only the addition of an occasional coal at the top. In fine establishments abroad, a grate for burning coal, charcoal, or wood is made in the kitchen, for the purpose of roasting only. This is convenient, but more expensive than roasting in ranges or stoves, where the same fire may serve for cooking every thing.

Sautéing.

As I have already said, frying implies immersing in fat or oil; but *sautéing* means to cook in a spider or *sauté* pan, with just enough hot fat to keep the article, while being cooked, from sticking. The fat should always be quite hot before placing on it any thing to cook.

Braising.

A braising-kettle has a deep cover, which holds coals; consequently, the cooking is done from above as well as below. It is almost air-tight, thus preventing evaporation, and the article to be cooked imbibes whatever flavor one may wish to give it.

The article is generally cooked in stock or broth (water may be used also), with slices of bacon, onion, carrot, etc., placed around the meat. It is a favorite mode of cooking pigeons. An ordinary cut of beef may be made very savory cooked in this manner, and the juice left makes a good gravy when freed from fat.

If a braising-pan is not at hand, a common, tight-covered saucepan answers very well without the upper coals. Except for coloring larding on the top of the article to be braised, I do not appreciate the value of the upper coals, anyway; and the coloring may be accomplished with the salamander or hot shovel as well.

Larding.

Cut the firmest bacon fat, with a heated or very sharp knife, into square lengths of equal size. Placing one end in a larding-needle, draw it through the skin and a small bit of the meat, leaving the strip of pork, or lardoon, as it is called, in the meat. The two ends left exposed should be of equal length. The punctures for the lardoons should be in rows, of equal distance apart, arranged in any fanciful way that may suit the cook. The usual form for larding, however, is as shown in cut (page 57).

Boning.

Boning is not a difficult operation. It only requires time, a thin, sharp knife, and a little care. Cut off the neck, and also the legs at the first joint. Cut the skin in a line down the middle of the back. Now, taking first one side and then the other of the cut in the fingers, carefully separate the flesh from the bones, sliding the knife close to the bone. When you come to the wings and legs, it is easier to break or unjoint the bones at the body-joint; cutting close by the bone, draw it, turning the flesh of the legs and wings inside out. When all the bones are out, the skin and flesh can be re-adjusted and stuffed into shape. As the leg and wing bones require considerable time to remove, they may be left in, and the body stuffed with lamb or veal force-meat. See receipt for boned chicken (page 174). It is a very pretty and delicious dish.

Egg and Bread Crumbing.

Always sift the bread or cracker crumbs. Whenever there are spare pieces or trimmings of bread or broken crackers, dry them at once in the oven, and after pounding and sifting, put them away in a tin can, for future use. In preparing for use, beat the eggs a little. If they are to be used for sweet dishes, such as rice croquettes, sweeten them slightly. If they are to be used for meats, sweet-breads, oysters, etc., always salt and pepper them, and for a change, finely chopped parsley may be added. Add a small proportion of milk to the eggs, say a half-cupful for two of them, or for one of them, if intended for fish or cutlets. Have the eggs in one plate, and the bread-crumbs in another; roll the article first in the crumbs, then in the egg, then in the crumbs again. In the case of articles very soft, like croquettes, it will be more convenient for one person to shape and roll them in the eggs, and another, with dry hands, to roll them in the bread-crumbs.

Pounded and sifted cracker-crumbs can be purchased by the pound, at bakeries and large groceries, for the same price as whole crackers. However, it will never be necessary to purchase cracker-crumbs, if all scraps of bread are saved and dried. It is deplorable for a cook to throw them away. It shows that she is either too indolent to ever learn to cook, or too ignorant of the uses of scraps of bread to be tolerated. If she saves them for purposes of charity, let her give fresh bread, which will be more acceptable, and save the scraps, which are equally useful to her. Yet if the bread-crumbs when pounded and sifted are not very fine, they are not as good as the cracker-dust.

To Cook Puddings in Boiling Water.

Wet and flour the cloth before adding the pudding. In tying in the pudding, leave room enough for it to swell. If cooked in a mold, do not fill the mold quite full. Never let the water stop boiling. As it wastes away in boiling, replenish the kettle from another containing boiling water.

It is better to cook these puddings (plum-puddings as well) in a steamer than in boiling water. The principle is really the same, and there is no water soaked.

Dried Celery, Parsley, etc., for Winter Use.

Celery, parsley, thyme, summer savory, sage, etc., should all be prepared for winter use. After drying and pulverizing, put them in tin cans or glass jars. Celery and parsley are especially valuable for soups and gravies.

Seeds for Soups.

If the fresh or dried vegetables are not at hand, seeds, such as celery, carrot-seed, etc., can be substituted for a flavoring.

To Flavor with Lemon Zest.

Never use the white part of the peel of a lemon for flavoring. It is bitter. The little globules of oil in the surface of the rind contain all the pleasant flavor of the peel. It may be thinly pared off, avoiding the white pulp. Professional cooks, however, rub loaf-sugar over the surface. The friction breaks the oil-ducts, and the sugar absorbs the oil. It is called zest. The sugar is afterward pounded fine for certain dishes, such as creams, *meringues*, etc.; or it can be simply melted in custards and beverages.

The Cook's Table of Weights and Measures.

1 quart of sifted flour = 1 pound.
1 quart of powdered sugar = 1 pound and 7 ounces.
1 quart of granulated sugar = 1 pound and 9 ounces.
1 pint of closely packed butter = 1 pound.
Butter, size of an egg = about 2 ounces.
10 eggs = 1 pound.
3 cupfuls of sugar = 1 pound.
5 cupfuls of sifted flour = 1 pound.
1 heaping table-spoonful = ⅙th of a gill.
4 gills = 1 pint; 2 pints = 1 quart; 4 quarts = 1 gallon.

In my receipts, I prefer, generally, the use of terms of measure to those of weight, because the former are more convenient for the majority of housekeepers.

To Chop Suet.

Sprinkle flour over it while chopping, which will prevent the pieces from adhering.

Rising-powder Proportions.

To 1 quart of flour, use 2½ tea-spoonfuls of baking-powder; or,

To 1 quart of flour, use 1 tea-spoonful of soda, and 2 tea-spoonfuls of cream of tartar; or,

To 1 quart of flour, use 1 cupful of sour milk, and 1 tea-spoonful of soda.

To Make Roux.

A *roux* is a mixture of butter and flour *cooked*. It is generally added, uncooked, to thicken a sauce or a soup; but the flavor is much better if it is first cooked, and the sauce or soup is added to *it*. Professional French cooks always manage it in this way. When the butter is first brought to the boiling-point, in a small stew-pan or cup, the sifted flour is sprinkled in, and both are mixed well together over the fire with an egg-whisk, until the flour is well cooked; a part of the sauce or soup is then stirred in until it becomes smooth and thin enough to add to the main sauce or soup. If the *roux* is intended for a white sauce, it is not allowed to color; if for a brown sauce, it may color a little, or browned flour may be used.

BREAD, AND BREAKFAST CAKES.

It requires experience to make good bread. One must know, first, how long to let the bread rise, as it takes a longer time in cold than in warm weather; second, when the oven is just of proper temperature to bake it. Bread should be put in a rather hot oven. It is nearly light enough to bake when put in; so the rule for baking bread differs from that of baking cake, which should be put into a moderate oven at first, to become equally heated through before rising. As bread requires a brisk heat, it is well to have the loaves small, the French-bread loaves being well adapted to a hot oven. After the bread is baked, the loaves should be placed on end (covered) at the back of the table until they become cool.

To Make Yeast.

Ingredients: A cupful of baker's yeast; four cupfuls of flour; two large potatoes, boiled; one cupful of sugar, and six cupfuls of boiling water.

Mix the warm mashed potatoes and sugar together; then add the flour; next, add the six cupfuls of boiling water, poured on slowly: this cooks the flour a little. It will be of the consistency of batter. Let the mixture get almost cold, stirring it well, that the bottom may become cool also. It will spoil the yeast if the batter be too hot. When lukewarm, add the tea-cupful of yeast. Leave this mixture in the kitchen, or in some warm place, perhaps on the kitchen-table (do not put it too near the stove), for five or six hours, until it gets perfectly light. Do not touch it until it gets somewhat light; then stir it down two or three times during the six hours. This process makes it stronger. Keep it in a cool place until needed.

This yeast will last perpetually, if a tea-cupful of it be always kept, when making bread, to make new yeast at the next baking. Keep it in a stone jar, scalding the jar every time fresh yeast is made.

In summer, it is well to mix corn-meal with the yeast, and dry it in cakes, in some shady, dry place, turning the cakes often, that they may become thoroughly dry. It requires about one and a half cakes (biscuit-cutter) to make four medium-sized loaves of bread. Crumb them, and let them soak in lukewarm water about a quarter or half an hour before using.

To make the Bread.

Ingredients: Flour, one and a half cupfuls of yeast, lukewarm water, a table-spoonful of lard, a little salt.

Put two quarts of flour into the bread-bowl; sprinkle a little salt over it; add one and a half cupfuls of yeast, and enough lukewarm water to make it a rather soft dough. Set it one side to rise. In winter, it will take overnight; in summer, about three hours. After it has risen, mix well into it one table-spoonful of lard; then add flour (not too much), and knead it half an hour. The more it is kneaded, the whiter and finer it becomes. Leave this in the bread-bowl for a short time to rise; then make it into loaves. Let it rise again for the third time. Bake.

Mrs. Bonner's Bread.

This is a delicious bread, which saves the trouble of making yeast. Twenty-five cents' worth of Twin Brothers' yeast will last a small family six weeks. I would recommend Mrs. Bonner's bread in preference to that of the last receipt. It is cheaper and better, at last, to always have good bread, which is insured by using fresh yeast each time.

For four loaves: At noon, boil three potatoes; mash them well; add a little salt, and two and a half cupfuls of flour; also enough boiling water (that in which the potatoes were boiled) to make rather a thin batter. Let it cool, and when it is at about blood-heat, add a Twin Brothers' yeast-cake, soaked in half a tea-cupful of lukewarm water. One yeast-cake will be sufficient for four loaves of bread in summer; but use one and a half yeast-cakes in winter. Stir well, and put it in a warm place. At night it will be light, when stir in enough flour to make the sponge. Do not make it too stiff. If you should happen to want a little more bread than usual, add a little warm water to the batter. Let it remain in a warm place until morning, when it should be well kneaded for at least twenty minutes. Half an hour or more would be better. Return the dough to the pan, and let it rise again. When light, take it out; add half a tea-spoonful of soda, dissolved in a table-spoonful of water; separate it into four loaves; put them in the pans, and let it rise again. When light, bake it an hour.

French Bread (*Grace Melaine Lourant*).

Put a heaping table-spoonful of hops and a quart of hot water over the fire to boil. Have ready five or six large boiled potatoes, which mash fine. Strain the hops. Now put a pint of boiling water (that in which the potatoes were boiled) over three cupfuls of flour; mix in the mashed potatoes, then the quart of strained hot hop-water, a heaping tea-spoonful of sugar, and the same of salt. When this is lukewarm, mix in one and a half Twin Brothers' yeast-cakes (softened). Let this stand overnight in a warm place.

In the morning, a new process is in order: First, pour over the yeast a table-spoonful of warm water, in which is dissolved half a spoonful of soda; mix in lightly about ten and a half heaping tea-cupfuls of sifted flour. No more flour is added to the bread during its kneading. Instead, the hands are wet in lukewarm water. Now knead the dough, giving it about eight or ten strokes; then taking it from the side next to you, pull it up into a long length, then double it, throwing it down *snappishly* and heavily. Wetting the hands again, give it the same number of strokes, or *kneads*, pulling the end toward you again, and throwing it over the part left in the pan. Continue this process until large bubbles are formed in the dough. It will take half an hour or longer. The hands should be wet enough at first to make the dough rather supple. If dexterously managed, it will not stick to the hands after a few minutes; and when it is kneaded enough, it will be very elastic, full of bubbles, and will not stick to the pan. When this time arrives, put the dough away again in a warm place to rise. This will take one or two hours.

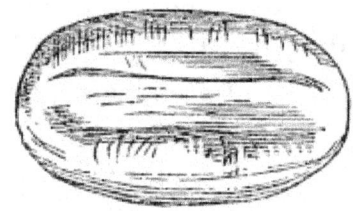

Now comes another new process. Sprinkle plenty of flour on the board, and take out lightly enough dough to make one loaf of bread, remembering that the French loaves are not large, nor of the same shape as the usual home-made ones. With the thumb and forefinger gather up the sides carefully (to prevent doubling the meshes or grain of the dough) to make it round in shape. Flour the rolling-pin, press it in the centre, rolling a little to give the dough the form of cut.

Now give each puffed end a roll toward the centre, lapping well the ends. Turn the bread entirely over, pulling out the ends a little, to give the loaf a long form, as in cut.

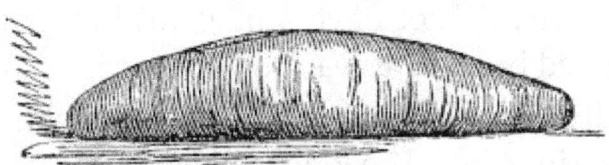

Sprinkle plenty of flour on large baking-pans turned bottom side up, upon which lay this and the other loaves, a little distance apart, if there is room for two of them on one pan. Sprinkle plenty of flour on the tops, and set the pans by the side of the fire to again rise a little. It will take twenty-five or thirty minutes longer. Then bake.

Kneading bread in the manner just described causes the *grain* of the bread to run in one direction, so that it may be pealed off in layers. Kneading with water instead of flour makes the bread moist and elastic, rather than solid and in crumbs.

Petits Pains

are made as in last receipt, by lightly gathering a little handful of dough, picking up the sides, and turning it over in the form of a ball or a biscuit. They are baked as described for French bread, placing them a little distance apart, so that they may be separate little breads, each one enough for one person at breakfast.

Toast.

I have remarked before that not one person in a thousand knows how to make good toast. The simplest dishes seem to be the ones oftenest spoiled. If the cook sends to the table a properly made piece of toast, one may judge that she is a *scientific* cook, and may entertain, at the same time, exalted hopes of her.

The bread should not be too fresh. It should be cut *thin*, evenly, and in good shape. The crust edges should be cut off. The pieces shaved off can be dried and put in the bread-crumb can. The object of toasting bread is to extract all its moisture—to convert the dough into pure farina of wheat, which is very digestible. Present each side of the bread to the fire for a few moments to *warm*, without attempting to toast it; then turn about the first side at some distance from the fire, so that it may slowly and evenly receive a *golden* color all over the surface. Now turn it to the other side, moving it in the same way, until it is perfectly toasted. The coals should be clear and hot. Serve it the moment it is done, on a warm plate, or, what is better, a toast-rack; consequently, do not have a piece of bread toasted until the one for whom it is intended is ready to eat it.

"If, as is generally done, a thick slice of bread is hurriedly exposed to a hot fire, and the exterior of the bread is toasted nearly black, the intention of extracting the moisture is defeated, as the heat will then produce no effect on the interior of the slice, which remains as moist as ever. Charcoal is a bad conductor of heat. The overtoasted surface is nothing more or less than a thin layer of charcoal, which prevents the heat from penetrating through the bread. Neither will butter pass through the hard surface: it will remain on it, and if exposed to heat, to melt it in, it will dissolve, and run over it in the form of rancid oil. *This* is why buttered toast is so often unwholesome."

DIXIE BISCUIT (*Mrs. Blair*).

Mix one tea-spoonful of salt into three pints of flour; put one tea-cupful of milk, with two table-spoonfuls of lard, on the fire to warm. Pour this on two eggs, well beaten; add the flour, with one tea-cupful of home-made yeast. When well mixed, set it in a warm place for about five hours to rise; then form into biscuit; let them rise again. Bake.

GRAHAM BREAD.

Make the sponge as for white bread; then knead in Graham flour, only sifting part of it. Add, also, two or three table-spoonfuls of molasses.

RUSKS.

Add to about a quart of bread dough the beaten yolks of three eggs, half a cupful of butter, and one cupful of sugar: mix all well together. When formed into little cakes (rather high and slender, and placed very near each other), rub the tops with sugar and water mixed; then sprinkle over dry sugar. This should fill two pans.

PARKER HOUSE ROLLS (*Mrs. Samuel Treat*).

Ingredients: Two quarts of flour, one pint of milk (measured after boiling), butter the size of an egg, one table-spoonful of sugar, one tea-cupful of home-made yeast, and a little salt.

Make a hole in the flour. Put in the other ingredients, in the following order: sugar, butter, milk, and yeast. Do not stir the ingredients after putting them together. Arrange this at ten o'clock at night; set it in a cool place until ten o'clock the next morning, when mix all together, and knead it fifteen minutes by the clock. Put it in a cool place again until four o'clock P.M., when cut out the rolls, and set each one apart from its neighbor in the pan. Set it for half an hour in a warm place. Bake fifteen minutes.

BEATEN BISCUIT.

Rub one quarter of a pound of lard into one and a half pounds of flour, adding a pinch of salt. Mix enough milk or water with it to make a *stiff* dough. Beat the dough well with a rolling-pin for half an hour or more, or until the dough will *break* when pulled. Little machines come for the purpose of making beaten biscuit, which facilitate the operation. Form into little biscuit, prick them on top several times with a fork, and bake.

SODA AND CREAM OF TARTAR BISCUIT.

Ingredients: One quart of flour, one tea-spoonful of soda, two tea-spoonfuls cream of tartar, one even tea-spoonful of salt, lard or butter the size of a small egg, and milk.

Put the soda, cream of tartar, and salt on the table; mash them smoothly with a knife, and mix well together; mix them as evenly in the flour as possible; then pass it all through the sieve two or three times. The success of the biscuits depends upon the equal distribution of these ingredients. Mix in the lard or butter (melted) as evenly as possible, taking time to rub it between the open hands, to break any little lumps. Now pour in enough milk to make the dough consistent enough to roll out, mixing it lightly with the ends of the fingers. The quicker it is rolled out, cut, and baked, the better will be the biscuits.

The biscuits are cheaper made with cream of tartar and soda than with baking-powder, yet many make the

BISCUITS WITH BAKING-POWDER.

They are made as in the last receipt, merely substituting two heaping tea-spoonfuls of baking-powder for the cream of tartar and soda, and taking the same care to mix evenly.

These biscuits are nice rolled quite thin (half an inch), and cut with a small cutter two inches in diameter. They may be served hot or cold, and are often used at evening companies, cold, split in two, buttered, and with chopped ham (as for sandwiches) placed between them. They are preferable to bread sandwiches, as they do not dry as quickly, and are, perhaps, neater to handle. These biscuits are especially nice when made with Professor Horsford's self-raising flour—of course, the raising powders are omitted. The appreciation of hot biscuits is quite a Southern and Western American fancy. They are rarely seen abroad, and are generally considered unwholesome in the Eastern States.

Muffins.

Ingredients: Two eggs, one pint of flour, one tea-cupful of milk or cream, butter half the size of an egg, a little salt, and one tea-spoonful of baking-powder.

Mix the baking-powder and salt in the flour. Beat the eggs; add to the yolks, first, milk, then butter (melted), then flour, then the whites. Beat well after it is all mixed, and bake them immediately in a hot oven, in gem-pans or rings. Take them out of the pans or rings the moment they are done, and send them to the table. The self-raising flour is very nice for making muffins. In using this, of course, the baking-powder should be omitted.

Waffles.

Ingredients: Two eggs, one pint of flour, one and a quarter cupfuls of milk or cream, one even tea-spoonful of yeast-powder, butter or lard the size of a walnut, and salt.

Mix the baking-powder and salt well in the flour, then rub in evenly the butter; next add the beaten yolks and milk mixed, then the beaten whites of the eggs. Bake immediately.

Rice Waffles (*Mrs. Gratz Brown*).

Ingredients: One and a half pints of boiled rice, one and a half pints of flour, half a tea-cupful of sour milk, half a tea-cupful of sweet milk, one tea-spoonful of soda, salt, three eggs, and butter size of a walnut.

Rice Pancakes

are made as in the last receipt, by adding an extra half-cupful of milk.

Hominy Cake (*Mrs. Watts Sherman*).

Add a spoonful of butter to two cupfuls of whole hominy (boiled an hour with milk) while it is still hot. Beat three eggs very light, which add to the hominy. Stir in gradually a pint of milk, and, lastly, a pint of corn-meal. Bake in a pan.

This is a very nice breakfast cake. Serve it, with a large napkin under it, on a plate. The sides of the napkin may cover the top of the cake until the moment of serving, which will keep it moist.

Baked Hominy Grits (*Mrs. Pope*).

Ingredients: One quart of milk, one cupful of hominy grits, two eggs, and salt.

When the milk is salted and boiling, stir in the hominy grits, and boil for twenty minutes. Set it aside to cool thoroughly. Beat the eggs to a stiff froth, and then beat them well and hard into the hominy. Bake half an hour.

Breakfast Puffs, or Pop-overs (*Mrs. Hopkins*).

Ingredients: Two cupfuls of milk, two cupfuls of flour, two eggs, and an even tea-spoonful of salt.

Beat the eggs separately and well, add the whites last, and then beat all well together. They may be baked in roll-pans, or deep gem-pans, which should be heated on the range, and greased before the batter is put in: they should be filled half full with the batter. Or they may be baked in tea-cups, of which eight would be required for this quantity of batter. When baked, serve immediately. For Graham gems use half Graham flour.

Henriettes for Tea (*French Cook*), No. 1.

Ingredients: Three eggs beaten separately, three-fourths of a cupful of cream or milk, a scant tea-spoonful of baking-powder, salt, one table-spoonful of brandy, a pinch of cinnamon, enough flour to make them just stiff enough to roll out easily.

Roll them thin as a wafer, cut them into about two-inch squares, or into diamonds, with the paste-jagger, fry them in boiling lard, and sprinkle over pulverized sugar.

Henriettes for Breakfast or Tea (*French Cook*), No. 2.

Ingredients: Three eggs beaten separately, one cupful of milk, a scant tea-spoonful of baking-powder, salt, one table-spoonful of brandy, and flour enough to make a little thicker than for pancakes.

Pass the batter through a funnel (one-third or one-half inch diameter at end) into hot boiling lard, making rings, or any figures preferred. Do not fry too much at one time. When done and drained, sprinkle over pulverized sugar, and lay them on a plate on a folded napkin. Serve.

Wafer Biscuits.

Rub a piece of butter the size of a large hickory-nut into a pint of sifted flour; sprinkle over a little salt. Mix it into a stiff, smooth paste, with the white of an egg beaten to a froth, and warm milk. Beat the paste with a rolling-pin for half an hour, or longer; the more the dough is beaten, the better are the biscuits. Form the dough into little round balls about the size of a pigeon's egg; then roll each of them to the size of a saucer. They should be mere wafers in thickness; they can not be too thin. Sprinkle a little flour over the tins. Bake.

These wafers are exceedingly nice to serve with a cheese course, or for invalids to eat with their tea.

Corn Bread.

Ingredients: One cupful of sour milk, one cupful of sweet milk, one table-spoonful of sugar or molasses, one tea-cupful of flour, two heaping tea-cupfuls of corn-meal, one tea-spoonful of salt, one tea-spoonful (not heaping) of soda, one and a half table-spoonfuls of melted lard or butter, and three eggs.

Beat the eggs separately; add the melted butter to the milk; then the sugar, salt, yolks, soda (dissolved in a table-spoonful of warm water); and, lastly, the whites, flour, and corn-meal. Beat it all quickly and well together. Put it immediately in the oven, to bake half an hour.

Hoe Cake.

Pour enough scalding water, or milk, on corn-meal (salted), to make it rather moist. Let it stand an hour, or longer. Put two or three heaping table-spoonfuls on a hot griddle, greased with pork or lard. Smooth over the surface, making the cake about half an inch thick, and of round shape. When browned on one side, turn and brown it on the other. Serve very hot.

These are very nice breakfast cakes, with a savory crust.

Corn Cake (*Mrs. Lackland*).

Ingredients: One pint of milk, half a pint of Indian meal, four eggs, a scant table-spoonful of butter, salt, and one tea-spoonful of sugar. Pour the milk boiling on the *sifted* meal. When cold, add the butter (melted), the salt, the sugar, the yolks of the eggs, and, lastly, the whites, well beaten separately. Bake half an hour in a hot oven. It is very nice baked in iron or tin gem-pans, the cups an inch and a half deep.

Fried Corn Mush for Breakfast.

Many slice the mush when cold, and simply *sauté* it in a little hot lard. But as some cooks seem to have as great success in simple dishes as in elaborate ones, I shall consider this as at least one of the little successes taught me by a French cook. Of course, the mush is made by sprinkling the corn-meal into *boiling salted* water, or after the manner of Harriet Plater, given in the next receipt. It is thoroughly cooked, and made the day before wanted. When cold, it is sliced, each slice dipped in beaten eggs (salted) and bread or cracker crumbs, and fried in boiling-hot lard. One should try this, to know the superiority in the manner of cooking.

Corn Mush

is usually made by sprinkling corn-meal into well-salted boiling water (a pint of corn-meal to three pints of water), and cooking it well. But Harriet Plater (Mrs. Filley's most skillful cook) says that corn-meal mush is much lighter, and when fried for breakfast, browns better by cooking it as follows:

"Put a quart of water on the fire to boil. Stir a pint of cold milk, with one pint of corn-meal and one tea-spoonful of salt. When the water boils, pour in the mixture gradually, stirring all well together. Let it boil for half an hour, stirring often, to prevent it from burning."

Oatmeal Porridge.

It seems very simple to make oatmeal porridge, yet it is a very different dish made by different cooks. The ingredients are: One heaping cupful of oatmeal to one quart of boiling water and one tea-spoonful of salt. Boil twenty minutes.

The water should be salted and boiling when the meal is sprinkled in with one hand, while it is lightly stirred in with the other. When all mixed, it should boil without afterward being stirred more than is necessary to keep it from burning at the bottom, and to mingle the grains two or three times, so that they may all be evenly cooked. If much stirred, the porridge will be starchy or waxy, and poor in flavor. But the puffing of the steam through the grains without much stirring swells each one separately, and, when done, the porridge is light, and quite consistent. This same manner of cooking is applicable as well to all other grains.

Mother Johnson's Pancakes (*Adirondacks*).

These are famous pancakes, and, like every other good thing, there is a little secret in the preparation.

Enough flour is added to a quart of sour milk to make a rather thick batter. The secret is that it is left to stand overnight, instead of being finished at once. It may even stand to advantage for twenty-four hours. However, if it is mixed at night, the next morning two well-beaten eggs and salt are to be added at the same time with half a tea-spoonful of soda, dissolved in a table-spoonful of warm water. Cook immediately.

Sirup.

Mix two table-spoonfuls of water to two cupfuls of brown sugar and one even table-spoonful of butter. Let it boil about five minutes.

Buckwheat Cakes.

Scald two gills of Indian meal in one quart of boiling water. Add a little salt. When cool, add one gill of yeast, and stir in enough buckwheat flour to make a thin batter. Let it rise overnight. If by chance it is a little sour, just before cooking add one-fourth of a tea-spoonful of soda, dissolved in half a cupful of boiling water. Or,

They may be made in the same manner without the Indian meal, merely adding the yeast to a quart of lukewarm water, and making the batter with buckwheat flour alone.

Pancakes, with Flour or Corn-meal.

Stir one or two cupfuls of cream or milk into two beaten eggs; add flour or corn-meal enough to make a thin batter. If the milk is sweet, add one tea-spoonful of yeast-powder; if it is sour, add, instead of the yeast-powder, half a tea-spoonful of soda, dissolved in a little warm water.

Pancakes, with Bread-crumbs.

Soak the bread-crumbs, then drain them. To two cupfuls of bread-crumbs add one cupful of flour or corn-meal, one egg, and milk enough to make a thin batter. If the milk is sweet, add a tea-spoonful of yeast-powder; if sour, half a tea-spoonful of soda, dissolved in a table-spoonful of warm water.

Strawberry Short-cake (*Mrs. Pope*).

Ingredients: One quart of flour, two heaping tea-spoonfuls of yeast-powder, half a tea-spoonful of salt, butter size of an egg, milk, two quarts of strawberries. Mix the baking-powder into the flour, then rub in the butter (in the same manner as described for biscuits, page 72). Add enough milk to make a soft dough—rather softer than for biscuits. Spread this on two pie-tins. Bake in a quick oven.

When the cakes are done, let them partly cool. Cut around the edges, and split them. Spread them with butter, then with one quart of mashed strawberries, with plenty of sugar; then put between them the other quart of whole strawberries, sprinkled with sugar. Serve a pitcher of cream with a strawberry short-cake. The cake in this form can be cut like a pie. It is a good summer breakfast as well as tea dish. Or,

It can be made with sour milk, viz.: to two tea-cupfuls of sour milk add a tea-spoonful of soda, then three-fourths of a tea-cupful of butter or lard, partly melted, and enough flour to make a soft dough. Roll it into thin cakes large enough to fill the pan in which they are to be baked. When baked, split, and butter them while hot. Lay on a plate half of the cake, put on a layer of well-sugared strawberries, then the other half, then more strawberries, and so on, until there are several layers. Or,

These cakes can be made in the same way with currants, blackberries, cut peaches, chopped pine-apples, raspberries, etc.

TEA.

Two things are necessary to insure good tea: first, that the water should be at the boiling-point when poured on the leaves, water simply hot not answering the purpose at all; and, second, that it should be served freshly made. Tea should never be boiled. So particular are the English to preserve its first aroma, that it is sometimes made on the table two or three times during a meal. In France, little silver canisters of tea are placed on the table, where it is invariably made. One tea-spoonful of the leaves is a fair portion for each person. Tea is better made in an earthen tea-pot, which tea connoisseurs are particular to have. They also drink the beverage without milk, and with loaf-sugar merely.

Water at the first boiling-point is generally considered better for tea or coffee, and, in fact, any kind of cooking which requires boiling water.

COFFEE.

The best coffee is made by mixing two-thirds Java and one-third Mocha. The Java gives strength, the Mocha flavor and aroma.

Coffee should be evenly and carefully roasted. Much depends upon this. If even a few of the berries are burned, the coffee will taste burned and bitter, instead of being fine-flavored and aromatic. To have the perfection of coffee, it should be fresh-roasted each day. Few, however, will take that trouble. As soon as it is roasted, and while still hot, stir into it one or two eggs, together with their shells (about one egg to a pint of roasted coffee-beans). This will help to preserve the coffee, as well as to make it clear. Put it away in a close-covered tin-case, and grind it only just before using.

Allow two heaping table-spoonfuls of ground coffee to a pint of water. Let the water be *boiling* when it is poured on the coffee. Cover it as tightly as possible, and boil it one minute; then let it remain a few moments at the side of the range to settle.

Delmonico allows one and a half pounds of coffee to one gallon of water. The coffee-pot, with a double base, is placed on the range in a vessel of hot water (*bain-marie*). The boiling water is poured over the coffee, which is contained in a felt strainer in the coffee-pot. It is not boiled.

Of course, much depends upon the care in preparing the coffee to insure a delicious beverage; but equally as much depends upon serving with it good thick cream. Milk, or even boiled milk, is not to be compared with cream. In cities, a gill, at least, might be purchased each morning for coffee, or a few table-spoonfuls might be saved from the evening's milk for at least *one* cup. Fill the cup two-thirds full, then, with hot, clear coffee, pour in one or two table-spoonfuls of cream, and use loaf-sugar.

Professor Blot, in his lectures, was very emphatic as to the impropriety of *boiling* coffee. He said by this means the aroma and flavor were carried into the attic, and a bitter decoction was left to be drunk. He preferred decidedly the coffee made in the French filter coffee-pot.

I have experimented upon coffee, and prefer it boiled for one minute in the ordinary coffee-pot. That made in the French filter is also most excellent. It is not boiled, and requires a greater proportion of coffee. But to be explicit, put the coffee in the filter. At the first boil of the water, pour one or two coffee-cupfuls of it on the coffee. Put back the water on the fire. When boiling again, pour on as much more, and repeat the process until the desired quantity is made.

CHOCOLATE (*Miss Sallie Schenck*).

Allow two sticks of chocolate to one pint of new milk. After the chocolate is scraped, either let it soak an hour or so, with a table-spoonful of milk to soften it, or boil it a few moments in two or three table-spoonfuls of water. Then, in either case, mash it to a smooth paste. When the milk, sweetened to taste with loaf-sugar, is boiling, stir in the chocolate-paste, adding a little of the boiling milk to it first, to dilute it evenly. Let it boil half a minute. Stir it well, or mill it, and serve immediately.

Maillard's chocolate is flavored with a little vanilla. The commoner brands, such as Baker's, will be nearly as good by adding a little vanilla when making. Miss Schenck (noted for her chocolate) adds a very little flavoring of brandy.

A very good addition, and one universally seen, when chocolate is served at lunch parties, is a heaping table-spoonful of whipped-cream, sweetened and flavored with a little vanilla before it is whipped, placed on the top of the chocolate in each cup, the cup being only three-quarters filled with the chocolate.

SOUP.

The meat should be fresh, lean (all fat possible being removed), and juicy to make the best soup. It is put into cold, clear water, which should be heated only moderately for the first half-hour. The object is to extract the juices of the meat, and if it be boiled too soon, the surface will become coagulated, thereby imprisoning the juice within. After the first half-hour the pot should be placed at the back of the stove, allowing the soup to simmer for four or five hours.

Nothing is more disagreeable at table than greasy soup. As all particles of fat are taken off hot liquor with some difficulty, soup should be made the day before it is to be used, when the fat will rise to the top and harden. It can then be easily removed.

When vegetables are used, they should be added only in time to become thoroughly done: afterward they absorb a portion of the richness of the soup.

When onions are used, they impart better flavor by being fried or *sautéd* in a little hot butter or other grease, before they are added to the soup. In fact, many professional cooks fry other vegetables also, such as carrots and turnips. Sometimes they even fry slightly the chickens, beef, etc., and then cut them into smaller pieces for boiling. Potatoes and cabbage should be boiled in separate water before they are added to a soup.

Amateur cooks seem to have a great aversion to making stock. They think it must be something troublesome, and too scientific to undertake; whereas, in truth, it saves the trouble of going through the process of soup-boiling every day, and it is as easy to make as any simple soup. One has only to increase the quantity of meat and bones to any desired proportion, adding pepper and salt, and also vegetables, if preferred.

The stock should be kept in a stone jar. It will form a jelly, and in cool weather will last at least a week.

Just before dinner each day, in order to prepare soup, it is only necessary to cut off some of the jelly and heat it. It is very good with nothing additional; but one can have a change of soup each day by adding different flavorings, such as onion, macaroni, vermicelli, tomato, tapioca, spring vegetables (which will make a *julienne*), poached eggs, fried bread, asparagus, celery, green pease, etc. I will be explicit about these additions in the receipts. Stock is also valuable for gravies, sauces, and stews, and for boiling many things, such as pigeons, chickens, etc.

Stock, or Pot au Feu.

In ordinary circumstances, beef alone, with some vegetables, will make a good broth or stock, in the proportion of two and a half pints of cold clear water to each pound of bones and meat; the bones and meat should be of about equal weight. It makes the soup more delicate to add chicken or veal. Chicken and veal together make a good soup, called *blond de veau*. Good soup can be made, also, by using the trimmings of fresh meat, bits of cold cooked beef, or the bones of any meat or fowl. In the choice of vegetables, onions (first fried or *sautéd*, and a clove stuck in), parsley, and carrots are oftenest used: turnips, parsnips, and celery should be employed more sparingly. The soup bunch at market is generally a very good distribution of vegetables. Nothing is more simple than the process of making stock or broth. Remember not to let it boil for the first half-hour; then it should simmer slowly and steadily, partly covered, for four or five hours. In royal kitchens the stock is cooked by gas. Skim frequently; as scum, if allowed to remain, gives an unpleasant flavor to the soup. Use salt sparingly, putting in a little at first, and seasoning at the last moment. Many a good soup is spoiled by an injudicious use of seasoning. Some add a few drops of lemon-juice to a broth. If wine or catsup is added, it should only be done at the last moment. Always strain the soup through a sieve or soup-strainer. Small scraps of meat or sediment look slovenly in a soup. Or,

A Simple Stock.

If you have no vegetables (you should always have them, especially onions and carrots, as they will keep), a very good stock can be made by employing the meat and bones alone, seasoned with pepper and salt. If rich enough, it might be served in this manner. However, it is a simple thing, about fifteen minutes before dinner, each day, to add a little boiled macaroni, fried onions, etc., to vary the soup.

Gouffé's Receipt for Stock, or Bouillon.

Three pounds of beef; one pound of bone (about the quantity in that weight of meat); five and a half quarts of clear cold water; two ounces of salt; two carrots, say ten ounces; two large onions, say ten ounces, with two cloves stuck in them; six leeks, say fourteen ounces; one head of celery, say one ounce; two turnips, say ten ounces; one parsnip, say two ounces.

Bouillon Served at Luncheons, Germans, etc.

Purchase about six pounds of beef and bone (soup bones) for ten persons. Cut up the meat and break the bones; add two quarts of cold water, and simmer slowly until all the strength is extracted from the meat. It will take about five hours. Strain it through a fine sieve, removing every particle of fat; and if there is more than ten cupfuls, reduce it by boiling to that quantity. Season only with pepper and salt.

It is served in bouillon cups at luncheons, at evening companies, Germans, etc.

Sometimes it is served clear and transparent, after the receipt for Amber Soup.

Amber Soup, or Clear Broth.

This soup is served at almost all company dinners. There can be no better choice, as a heavy soup is not then desirable.

Ingredients: A large soup bone (say two pounds), a chicken, a small slice of ham, a soup bunch (or an onion, two sprigs of parsley, half a small carrot, half a small parsnip, half a stick of celery), three cloves, pepper, salt, a gallon of cold water, whites and shells of two eggs, and caramel for coloring.

Let the beef, chicken, and ham boil slowly for five hours; add the vegetables and cloves, to cook the last hour, having first fried the onion in a little hot fat, and then in it stuck the cloves. Strain the soup into an earthen bowl, and let it remain overnight. Next day remove the cake of fat on the top; take out the jelly, avoiding the settlings, and mix into it the beaten whites of the eggs with the shells. Boil quickly for half a minute; then, placing the kettle on the hearth, skim off carefully all the scum and whites of the eggs from the top, not stirring the soup itself. Pass this through the jelly bag, when it should be quite clear. The soup may then be put aside, and reheated just before serving. Add then a large table-spoonful of caramel, as it gives it a richer color, and also a slight flavor.

Of course, the brightest and cleanest of kettles should be used. I once saw this transparent soup served in Paris, without color, but made quite thick with tapioca. It looked very clear, and was exceedingly nice.

This soup may be made in one day. After it is strained, add the eggs and proceed as in receipt. However, if it is to be served at a company dinner, it is more convenient to make it the day before.

To make Caramel, or Burned Sugar, for coloring Broth.

The appearance of broth is improved by being of a rich amber color. The most innocent coloring substance, which does not impair the flavor of the broth, is caramel, prepared as follows:

Put into a porcelain saucepan, say half a pound of sugar, and a tablespoonful of water. Stir it constantly over the fire until it has a bright, dark-brown color, being very careful not to let it burn or blacken. Then add a teacupful of water and a little salt; let it boil a few moments longer; cool and strain it. Put it away in a close-corked bottle, and it is always ready for coloring soups.

Thickenings for Soup.

I have before recommended the making of soup the day before it is served, as this is the best means of having it entirely free from fat and settlings. Just before it is served, it may be thickened with corn starch, sago, tapioca, pearl barley, rice, etc. If a thickening of flour is used, let it be a *roux*, mixed according to directions, page 51. However, a rich stock jelly needs no thickening.

Additions To Beef Stock, to form Other Kinds of Soup.

It is well, just before the beef soup is sent to table, to drop into the tureen poached eggs, which have been cooked in salted water, and neatly trimmed. There may be an egg for each person at table. This is a favorite soup in Havana. Or, Put into the tureen, just before the soup is sent to table, slices of lemon—one slice for each plate. Or,

Yolks of hard-boiled eggs, one for each person. Or,

Put into the tureen *croûtons* or dice of bread, say three-quarters of an inch square, fried in a little butter. When frying, or rather *sautéing*, turn them, that all sides may be browned. They may be prepared several hours, if more convenient, before dinner; then left near the fire, to become crisp and dry. This makes a very good soup, and is also an excellent means of using dry bread. It is a favorite French soup, called *potage aux croûtons*. Or,

Drop into the tureen force-meat balls.

Receipt for Force-meat Balls.

Take any kind of meat or chicken, or both (that used for making the soup will answer); chop it very fine; season it with pepper, salt, a little chopped parsley and thyme, or a little parsley and fried onion, or with thyme, or parsley alone, a little lemon-juice, and grated peel. Break in a raw egg, and sprinkle over some flour; roll them in balls the size of a pigeon's egg. Fry or *sauté* them in a little butter, or they may be cooked in boiling water; or they may be egged and bread-crumbed, and fried in boiling lard. This is the most simple receipt. The French take much trouble in making *quenelles*, etc., for soup. Or,

A simple and delicious addition is that of four or five table-spoonfuls of stewed tomatoes.

Macaroni Soup

is only an addition of macaroni to the stock-jelly. However, boil the macaroni first in salted water. When done, drain it, and cut it into about two or three inch lengths. Put these pieces into the soup when it is simmering on the fire, then serve it a few minutes after. Many send, at the same time, a plate of grated cheese. This is passed, a spoon with it, after the plates of soup are served, each person adding a spoonful of it to their soup, if they choose. They probably will not choose it a second time.

Vermicelli Soup

is made exactly as macaroni soup, only the vermicelli is not cut, and, if *very little* of it is used, it may be boiled in the soup. Often the stock for vermicelli is preferred made of veal and chicken, instead of beef; however, either is very good. Grated cheese may also be served with it.

Noodles (*Eleanore Bouillotat*).

Three delicious dishes may be made from this simple and economical receipt for noodles:

To three eggs (slightly beaten), two table-spoonfuls of water, and a little salt, add enough flour to make a rather stiff dough; work it well for fifteen or twenty minutes, as you would dough for crackers, adding flour when necessary. When pliable, cut off a portion at a time, roll it thin as a wafer, sprinkle over flour, and, beginning at one side, roll it into a rather tight roll. With a sharp knife, cut it, from the end, into very thin slices (one-eighth inch), forming little wheels or curls. Let them dry an hour or so. Part may be used to serve as a vegetable, part for a noodle soup, and the rest should be dried, to put one side to use at any time for a beef soup.

To serve as a Vegetable.

Three cupfuls of fresh noodles, three quarts of salted boiling water, bread-crumbs, butter size of an egg.

Throw a few of the noodles at a time into the boiling salted water, and boil them until they are done, separating and shaking them with a large fork to prevent them from matting together. Skin them out when done, and keep them on a warm dish in a warm place until enough are cooked in a similar manner. Now mix the butter (in which the bread-crumbs were fried) evenly in them; put them on the platter on which they are to be served, and sprinkle over the top bread-crumbs fried or *sautéd* in some hot butter until they are of a light-brown color. This is a very good dish to serve with a fish, or with almost any meat, or it can be served as a course by itself; or the noodles can be cooked as macaroni, with cheese.

Noodle Soup.

Add to the water in which the noodles were boiled, as in last receipt, part of the butter in which the bread-crumbs were *sautéd*, a table-spoonful of chopped parsley, and two or three table-spoonfuls of the cooked noodles. Season with more salt, if necessary. Serve.

Beef Noodle Soup.

Add to a beef stock a small handful of fresh or dried noodles about twenty minutes before serving, which will be long enough time to cook them.

Many varieties of soups may be made by adding different kinds of vegetables to beef soup or stock. Cauliflower, cabbage, potatoes, and asparagus are better boiled in separate water, and added to the soup-tureen at the last moment. Onions, leeks, turnips, and carrots are better fried to a light color in a *sauté* pan with a little butter or clarified grease, and added to the soup. In frying, it is better to accompany the vegetable or vegetables with a little onion.

If you add more onion, more turnip, or more carrot than any other vegetable, you have onion, turnip, or carrot soup. I will specify a few combinations of vegetables.

Spring Soup.

A stock with any spring vegetables added which have first been parboiled in other water. Those generally used are pease, asparagus-tops, or a few young onions or leeks. This soup is often colored with caramel. Or,

Here is Francatelli's receipt for spring soup, a little simplified: Cut with a vegetable-cutter two carrots and two turnips into little round shapes; add the white part of a head of celery; twelve small young onions, sliced, without the green stalks; and one head of cauliflower, cut into flowerets. Parboil these vegetables for three minutes in boiling water. Drain, and add them to two quarts of stock, made of chicken or beef (chicken is better). Let the whole simmer gently for half an hour, then add the white leaves of a head-lettuce (cut the size of a half-dollar, with a cutter). As soon as tender, and when about to send the soup to the table, add half a gill of small green pease, and an equal quantity of asparagus-heads, which have been previously boiled in other water.

Julienne Soup, with Poached Eggs (*Dubois*).

Take two medium-sized carrots, a medium-sized turnip, a piece of celery, the core of a lettuce, and an onion. Cut them into thin fillets about an inch long. Fry the onion in butter over a moderate fire, without allowing it to take color; add the carrots, turnips, and celery—raw, if tender; if not, boil them separately for a few minutes. After frying all slowly for a few moments, season with a pinch of salt and a tea-spoonful of powdered-sugar. Then moisten them with a gill of broth, and boil until reduced to a glaze. Now add nearly two quarts of good stock, which has been skimmed and passed through a sieve, and remove the stew-pan to the back of the stove, so that the soup may boil only partially. A quarter of an hour after add the lettuce (which has been boiled in other water), and a few raw sorrel leaves, if they can be procured. This soup is quite good enough without eggs, yet they are a pleasant addition. Poach them in salted water, trim them, and drop into the soup-tureen just as it is ready to send to the table. Many color this soup with caramel. In that case, the sugar should be omitted.

Asparagus Soup.

Ingredients: Three pints of beef soup or stock, thirty heads of asparagus, a little cream, butter, flour, and a little spinach.

Cut the tops off the asparagus, about half an inch long, and boil the rest. Cut off all the tender portions, and rub them through a sieve, adding a little salt. Warm three pints of stock, add a *roux* made of a small piece of butter and a heaping tea-spoonful of flour; then add the asparagus pulp. Boil it slowly a quarter of an hour, stirring in two or three table-spoonfuls of cream. Color the soup with a tea-spoonful of spinach green, and, just before serving it, add the asparagus-tops, which have been separately boiled.

Many like this soup, but I prefer simply boiled asparagus-points added to stock or beef soup, just before serving.

Spinach Green.

Pound some spinach well, adding a few drops of water; squeeze the juice through a cloth, and put it on a strong fire. As soon as it looks curdy, take it off, and strain the liquor through a sieve. What remains on the sieve will be the coloring matter.

Ox-tail Soup.

Ox-tails make an especially good soup, on account of the gelatinous matter they contain.

Ingredients: Two ox-tails, a soup bunch, or a good-sized onion, two carrots, one stalk of celery, a little parsley, and a small cut of pork.

Cut the ox-tails at the joints, slice the vegetables, and mince the pork. Put the pork into a stew-pan. When hot, add first the onions; when they begin to color, add the ox-tails. Let them fry or *sauté* a very short time. Now cut them to the bone, that the juice may run out in boiling. Put both the ox-tails and fried onions into a soup kettle, with four quarts of cold water. Let them simmer for about four hours; then add the other vegetables, with three cloves stuck in a little piece of onion, and pepper and salt. As soon as the vegetables are well cooked, the soup is done. Strain it. Select some of the joints (one for each plate), trim them, and serve them with the soup. Or, if preferred, the joints may be left out.

CHICKEN SOUP (*Potage à la Reine*).—*Francatelli.*

Roast a large chicken. Clear all the meat from the bones, chop, and pound it thoroughly with a quarter of a pound of boiled rice. Put the bones (broken) and the skin into two quarts of cold water. Let it simmer for some time, when it will make a weak broth. Strain it, and add it to the chicken and rice. Now press this all through a sieve, and put it away until dinner-time. Take off the grease on top; heat it without boiling, and, just before sending to table, mix into it a gill of boiling cream. Season carefully with pepper and salt.

PURÉE OF CHICKEN (*Giuseppe Romanii*).

Chef de Cuisine of the Cooking-school in New York.

Ingredients: One and a half pounds of chicken, one and a half quarts of white stock (made with veal), half a sprig of thyme, two sprigs of parsley, half a blade of mace, one shallot, a quarter of a pound of rice, and half a pint of cream.

Roast the chicken, and when cold cut off all the flesh; put the bones into the white stock, together with the thyme, mace, parsley, shallot, and washed rice; boil it until the rice is very thoroughly cooked. In the mean time, chop the chicken; pound it in a mortar; then pass it through a sieve or colander, helping the operation by moistening it with a little of the stock. Strain the balance of the stock, allowing the rice to pass through the sieve.

Half an hour before dinner, add the chicken to the stock and heat it *without boiling*. Just before serving, add to it half a pint of boiling cream. Season with pepper and salt.

Plain Chicken Soup.

Cut up the chicken, and break all the bones; put it in a gallon of cold water; let it simmer for five hours, skimming it well. The last hour add, to cook with the soup, a cupful of rice and a sprig of parsley. When done, let the kettle remain quiet a few moments on the kitchen table, when skim off every particle of fat with a spoon. Then pour all on a sieve placed over some deep dish. Take out all the bones, pieces of meat, and parsley. Press the rice through the sieve. Now mix the rice, by stirring it with the soup, until it resembles a smooth *purée*. Season with pepper and salt.

Giblet Soup.

This soup is a great success. It is very inexpensive, a plate of giblets only costing at market five cents. It is a very good imitation of mock-turtle soup, and, after the first experience in making, it will be found very easy to manage.

Ingredients: The giblets of four chickens or two turkeys, one medium-sized onion, one small carrot, half a turnip, two sprigs of parsley, a leaf of sage, eggs, a little lemon-juice, Port or Madeira wine, and one or two cupfuls of chicken or beef stock, quite strong.

Cut up the vegetables. Put a piece of butter the size of a small egg into a stew-pan. When quite hot, throw in the sliced onion. When they begin to brown, add the carrot and turnip, a table-spoonful of flour, and the giblets. Fry them all quickly for a minute, watching them constantly, that the flour may brown, and not burn. Now cut the giblets (that the juice may escape), and put all into the soup-kettle, with a little pepper and salt, and three quarts of water—of course, stock would be much better, and for extra occasions I would recommend it; or without stock, one could add any fresh bones or scraps of lean meat one might happen to have. Pieces of chicken are especially well adapted to this soup; yet, for ordinary occasions, giblets alone answer very well.

Let the soup simmer for five hours; then strain it. Thicken it a little with *roux* (page 51), letting the flour brown, and add to it also one of the livers mashed. Season with the additional pepper and salt it needs, a little lemon-juice, and two table-spoonfuls of Port or Madeira wine. Put into the soup tureen yolks of hard-boiled eggs, one for each person at table. Pour over the soup, and serve.

Mock-turtle Soup (*New York Cooking-school*).

Let some one beside yourself remove the flesh from a calf's head, viz., cut from between the ears to the nose, touching the bone; then, cutting close to it, take off all the flesh. Turn over the head, cut open the jaw-bone from underneath, and take out the tongue whole. Turn the head back again, crack the top of the skull between the ears, and take out the brains whole; they may be saved for a separate dish. Soak all separately for a few moments in salt and water. Cut the skull all to pieces, wash it quickly, and put it on the fire in four quarts of cold water, together with the flesh, tongue, half a bunch of parsley, half a stalk of celery, one large bay-leaf, three cloves, half an inch of a stick of cinnamon, six whole allspice, six pepper-corns, half of a large carrot, and one turnip. When the tongue is tender, take it out, to be served as a separate dish (with spinach or with *sauce Tartare*). Leave in the flesh for about two hours, when it will be perfectly tender. Let the bones, etc., simmer for six hours, then strain, and put it away until the next day.

At the same time that the calf's head is cooking in one vessel, make a stock in another, with a beef or veal soup-bone (two or three pounds), and any scraps of poultry (it would be improved with a chicken added; and one might take this opportunity to have a boiled chicken for dinner, cooking it in the stock), put into two or three quarts of water, and simmered until reduced to a pint.

The next day, remove the fat and settlings from the two stocks.

Put into a two-quart stew-pan two ounces of butter (size of an egg), and, when it bubbles, stir in an ounce of ham cut in strips, and one heaping table-spoonful of flour (one and a half ounces). Stir it constantly until it gets quite brown, pour the reduced stock over it, mix it well, and strain it.

Now to half a pound of the calf's head cut in dice add one quart of the calf's-head stock boiling hot, and the pint of reduced and thickened stock, the juice of half a lemon, and one glassful of sherry. When it is about to boil, set it one side, and skim it very carefully. Add the flesh cut from the head, cut in dice, and two hard-boiled eggs cut in dice, and salt. Or,

Receipt for Egg-balls.—If, instead of the egg-dice, egg-balls should be preferred, add to the yolks of two hard-boiled eggs the raw yolk of one egg, one table-spoonful of melted butter, a little salt and pepper, and enough sifted flour to make it consistent enough to handle. Sprinkle flour on the board, roll it out about half an inch thick, cut it into dice, and roll each one into little balls in the palm of the hand. Put these into the soup five minutes before it is served, to cook. Or,

Receipt for Meat-balls.—If, instead of meat-dice, meat-balls should be preferred, to three-fourths of a cupful of the head-meat, chopped very fine, add a pinch of thyme, the grated peel of half a lemon, one raw egg, and flour enough to bind all together. Form into little balls the size of a hickory-nut; *sauté* them in a little hot butter. Or, It is very nice to add, instead of egg-balls, whole yolks of hard-boiled eggs, one for each plate.

The brains may be used for making croquettes (page 176), or as in receipt (page 151).

A SIMPLE MOCK-TURTLE SOUP.

Put four pig's feet, or calf's feet, and one pound of veal into four quarts of cold water, and let it simmer for five hours, reducing it to two quarts. Strain it, and let it remain overnight. The next day skim off the fat from the top, and remove the settlings from the bottom.

About half an hour before dinner put the soup on the fire, and season it with half a tea-spoonful of powdered thyme, a salt-spoonful of mace, a salt-spoonful of ground cloves. Simmer it for ten minutes. Now make a *roux* in a saucepan, viz.: put in one ounce of butter (size of a walnut), and, when it bubbles, sprinkle in one and a half ounces of flour (one table-spoonful). Stir it until the flour assumes a light-brown color; add the soup, and stir all together with the egg-whisk.

Make force-meat balls as follows: Chop some of the veal (used to make the soup), and about a quarter as much suet, very fine; season it with salt and pepper, and a few drops of lemon-juice; bind all together with some raw yolks of eggs and some cracker or bread crumbs; mold them into little balls about the size of a pigeon's egg, or smaller, if preferred. Fry them in boiling lard, or boil them two or three minutes in water. Cut up also some of the meat, or rather skin and cartilaginous substance, from the cold feet, which resembles turtle meat. Now put into the soup-tureen these meat-balls, pieces of calf's feet, and some yolks entire, or slices of hard-boiled eggs.

Season the soup the last minute with a little lemon-juice and one or two table-spoonfuls of sherry.

For a small family, this will make soup enough for two dinners.

Gumbo Soup.

Ingredients: One large chicken; one and a half pints of green gumbo, or one pint of dried gumbo; three pints of water; pepper and salt.

Cut the chickens into joints, roll them in flour, and fry or *sauté* them in a little lard. Take out the pieces of chicken, and put in the sliced gumbo (either the green or the dried), and *sauté* that also until it is brown. Drain well the chickens and gumbo. There should be about a table-spoonful of brown fat left in the *sauté* pan; to this add a large table-spoonful of browned flour; then add the three pints of water, the chicken, cut into small pieces, and the gumbo. Simmer all together two hours. Strain through a colander. Serve boiled rice in another dish by the side of the soup-tureen. Having put a ladleful of the soup in the soup-plate, place a table-spoonful of rice in the centre.

Gumbo and Tomato Soup.

If canned gumbo and tomatoes mixed are used, merely add to them a pint or more of stock or strong beef broth. Bring them to the boiling-point, and season with pepper and salt.

If the fresh vegetables are used, boil the tomatoes and gumbo together for about half an hour, first frying the gumbo in a little hot lard. Many, however, boil the gumbo without frying.

Mullagatawny Soup (*an Indian soup*).

Cut up a chicken; put it into a soup-kettle, with a little sliced onion, carrot, celery, parsley, and three or four cloves. Cover it with four quarts of water. Add any pieces of veal, with the bones, you may have; of course, a knuckle of veal would be the proper thing. When the pieces of chicken are nearly done, take them out, and trim them neatly, to serve with the soup. Let the veal continue to simmer for three hours.

Now fry an onion, a small carrot, and a stick of celery sliced, in a little butter. When they are a light brown, throw in a table-spoonful of flour; stir it on the fire one or two minutes; then add a good tea-spoonful of curry powder, and the chicken and veal broth. Place this on the fire to simmer the usual way for an hour. Half an hour before dinner, strain the soup, skim off all the fat, return it to the fire with the pieces of chicken, and two or three table-spoonfuls of boiled rice. This will give time enough to cook the chickens thoroughly.

Oyster Soup.

To one quart, or twenty-five oysters, add a half pint of water. Put the oysters on the fire in the liquor. The moment it begins to simmer (not *boil*, for that would shrivel the oysters), pour it through a colander into a hot dish, leaving the oysters in the colander. Now put into the saucepan two ounces of butter (size of an egg); when it bubbles, sprinkle in a table-spoonful (one ounce) of sifted flour; let the *roux* cook a few moments, stirring it well with the egg-whisk; then add to it gradually the oyster-juice, and half a pint of good cream (which has been brought to a boil in another vessel); season carefully with Cayenne pepper and salt; skim well, then add the oysters. Do not let it boil, but serve immediately. An oyster soup is made with thickening; an oyster stew is made without it (see receipt).

Oyster crackers and pickles are often served with an oyster soup.

Clam Soup.

To extract the clams from the shells, wash them in cold water, and put them all into a large pot over the fire, containing half a cupful of boiling water; cover closely, and the steam will cause the clams to open; pour all into a colander over a pan, and extract the meat from the shells.

Put a quart of the clams with their liquor on the fire, with a pint of water; boil them about three minutes, during which time skim them well, then strain them. Beard them, and return the liquor to the fire, with the hard portions of the clams (keeping the soft portions aside in a warm place), half an onion (one ounce), a sprig of thyme, three or four sprigs of parsley, and one large blade of mace; cover it, and let it simmer for half an hour.

In the mean time make a *roux*, *i. e.*, put three ounces of butter (size of an egg) into a stew-pan, and when it bubbles sprinkle in two ounces of flour (one heaping table-spoonful); stir it on the fire until cooked, and then stir in gradually a pint of hot cream; add this to the clam liquor (strained), with a seasoning of salt and a little Cayenne pepper; also the soft clams, without chopping them. When well mixed, and thoroughly hot (without boiling), serve immediately.

Bean Soup.

Soak a quart of navy beans overnight. Then put them on the fire, with three quarts of water; three onions, fried or *sautéd* in a little butter; one little carrot; two potatoes, partly boiled in other water; a small cut of pork; a little red pepper, and salt. Let it all boil slowly for five or six hours. Pass it then through a colander or sieve. Return the pulp to the fire; season properly with salt and Cayenne pepper. Put into the tureen *croûtons*, or bread, cut in half-inch squares, and fried brown on all sides in a little butter or in boiling fat. Professor Blot adds broth, bacon, onions, celery, one or two cloves, and carrot to his bean soup. A French cook I once had added a little mustard to her bean soup, which made a pleasant change. Another cook adds cream at the last moment. Or,

A very good bean soup can be made from the remains of baked beans; the brown baked beans giving it a good color. Merely add water and a bit of onion; boil it to a pulp, and pass it through the colander.

If a little stock, or some bones or pieces of fresh meat are at hand, they add also to the flavor of bean soup.

Bean and Tomato Soup.

A pint of canned tomatoes, boiled, and passed through the sieve, with a quart of bean soup, makes a very pleasant change.

Onion Soup (*Soupe à l'Ognon*).

A soup without meat, and delicious.

I was taught how to make this soup by a Frenchwoman; and it will be found a valuable addition to one's culinary knowledge. It is a good Friday soup.

Put into a saucepan butter size of a pigeon's egg. Clarified grease, or the cakes of fat saved from the top of stock, or soup (I always use the latter), answer about as well. When very hot, add two or three large onions, sliced thin; stir, and cook them well until they are red; then add a full half-teacupful of flour. Stir this also until it is red, watching it constantly, that it does not burn. Now pour in about a pint of boiling water, and add pepper and salt. Mix it well, and let it boil a minute; then pour it into the soup-kettle, and place it at the back of the range until almost ready to serve. Add then one and a half pints or a quart of boiling milk, and two or three well-mashed boiled potatoes. Add to the potatoes a little of the soup at first, then more, until they are smooth, and thin enough to put into the soup-kettle. Stir all well and smoothly together; taste, to see if the soup is properly seasoned with pepper and salt, as it requires plenty, especially of the latter. Let it simmer a few moments. Put pieces of toasted bread (a good way of using dry bread), cut in diamond shape, in the bottom of the tureen. Pour over the soup, and serve very hot. Or,

This soup might be made without potatoes, if more convenient, using more flour, and all milk instead of a little water. However, it is better with the potato addition; or it is much improved by adding stock instead of water; or, if one should chance to have a boiled chicken, the water in which it was boiled might be saved to make this soup.

Vegetable Soup without Meat (*Purée aux Légumes*).

Cut up a large plateful of any and all kinds of vegetables one happens to have; for example, onions, carrots, potatoes (boiled in other water), beans (of any kind), parsnips, celery, pease, parsley, leeks, turnips, cauliflower, spinach, cabbage, etc., always having either potatoes or beans for a thickening. First put into a saucepan half a tea-cupful of butter (clarified suet or stock-pot fat is just as good). When it is very hot, put in first the cut-up onions. Stir them well, to prevent from burning. When they assume a fine red color, stir in a large table-spoonful of flour until it has the same color. Now stir in a pint of hot water, and some pepper and salt. Mind not to add pepper and salt at first, as the onions and flour would then more readily burn. Add, also, all the other vegetables. Let them simmer (adding more hot water when necessary) for two hours; then press them through a colander. Return them to the range in a soup-kettle, and let them simmer until the moment of serving.

Corn Soup.

This is a very good soup, made with either fresh or canned corn. When it is fresh, cut the corn from the cob, and scrape off well all that sweetest part of the corn which remains on the cob. To a pint of corn add a quart of hot water. Boil it for an hour or longer; then press it through the colander. Put into the saucepan butter the size of a small egg, and when it bubbles sprinkle in a heaping table-spoonful of sifted flour, which cook a minute, stirring it well. Now add half of the corn pulp, and, when smoothly mixed, stir in the remainder of the corn: add Cayenne pepper, salt, a scant pint of boiling milk, and a cupful of cream.

This soup is very nice with no more addition, as it will have the pure taste of the corn; yet many add the yolks of two eggs just before serving, mixed with a little milk or cream, and not allowed to boil. Others add a table-spoonful of tomato catsup.

Tomato Soup, with Rice.

Cut half a small onion into rather coarse slices, and fry them in a little hot butter in a *sauté* pan. Add to them then a quart can, or ten or eleven large tomatoes cut in pieces, after having skinned them, and also two sprigs of parsley. Let it cook about ten minutes, when remove the pieces of onion and parsley. Pass the tomato through a sieve. Put into the stew-pan butter the size of a pigeon's egg, and when it bubbles sprinkle in a tea-spoonful of flour; when it has cooked a minute, stir in the tomato pulp: season with pepper and salt. It is an improvement to add a cupful or more of stock; however, if it is not at hand, it may be omitted.

Return the soup to the fire, and, when quite hot, add a cupful of fresh-boiled rice and half a tea-spoonful of soda.

Tomato Soup (*Purée aux Tomates*).—*Mrs. Corbett.*

Boil a dozen or a can of tomatoes until they are very thoroughly cooked, and press them through a sieve. To a quart of tomato pulp add a tea-spoonful of soda. Put into a saucepan butter the size of a pigeon's egg, and when it bubbles sprinkle and stir in a heaping tea-spoonful of flour. When it is cooked, stir into this a pint of hot milk, a little Cayenne pepper, salt, and a handful of cracker crumbs. When it boils, add the tomato pulp. Heat it well without boiling, and serve immediately.

The soda mixed with the tomatoes prevents the milk from curdling.

Sorrel Soup (*Soupe à la Bonne Femme*).

This is a most wholesome soup, which would be popular in America if it were better known. It is much used in France. Sorrel can be obtained, in season, at all the French markets in America.

For four quarts of soup, put into a saucepan a piece of butter the size of an egg, two or three sprigs of parsley, two or three leaves of lettuce, one onion, and a pint of sorrel (all finely chopped), a little nutmeg, pepper, and salt. Cover, and let them cook or sweat ten minutes; then add about two table-spoonfuls of flour. Mix well, and gradually add three quarts of boiling water (stock would be better). Make a *liaison, i. e.*, beat the yolks of four eggs (one egg to a quart of soup), and mix with them a cupful of cream or rich milk.

Add a little chevril (if you have it) to the soup; let it boil ten minutes; then stir in the eggs, or *liaison*, when the soup is quite ready.

Potato Soup (No. 1).

Fry seven or eight potatoes and a small sliced onion in a *sauté* pan in some butter or drippings—stock-pot fat is most excellent for this purpose. When they are a little colored, put them into two or three pints of hot water (stock would, of course, be better; yet hot water is oftenest used); add also a large heaping table-spoonful of chopped parsley. Let it boil until the potatoes are quite soft. Put all through the colander. Return the *purée* to the fire, and let it simmer two or three minutes. When just ready to serve, take the kettle off the fire; add plenty of salt and pepper, and the beaten yolks of two or three eggs. Do not let the soup boil when the eggs are in, as they would curdle.

Potato Soup (No. 2).

A very good soup for one which seems to have nothing in it.

Peel and cut up four rather large potatoes. When they are nearly done, pour off the water, and add one quart of hot water. Boil two hours, or until the potatoes are thoroughly dissolved in the water. Add fresh boiling water as it boils away. When done, run it through the colander, adding three-fourths of a cupful of hot cream, a large table-spoonful of finely cut parsley, salt, and pepper. Bring it to the boiling-point, and serve.

Purée of String-beans.

Make a strong stock as follows: Add to a knuckle of veal three quarts of water, a generous slice of salt pork, and two or three slices of onion. Let it simmer for five hours, then pour it through a sieve or colander into a jar. It is better to make this stock the day before it is served, as then every particle of fat may be easily scraped off the jelly.

Ten minutes before dinner, put into a saucepan two ounces of butter, and when it bubbles sprinkle in four ounces of flour (two heaping table-spoonfuls); let it cook without taking color; then add a cupful of hot cream, a pint of the heated stock, and about a pint of green string-bean pulp, *i. e.*, either fresh or canned string-beans boiled tender with a little pork, then pressed through a colander, and freed from juice. After mixing all together, do not let the soup boil, or it will curdle and spoil. Stir it constantly while it is on the fire.

Just before it is sent to table, sprinkle over the top a handful of little fried fritter-beans. They are made by dropping *drops* of fritter batter into boiling lard. They will resemble navy-beans, and give a very pleasant flavor and appearance to the soup.

If this pretty addition be considered too much trouble, little dice of fried bread (*croûtons*) may be added instead. The soup should be rather thick, and served quite hot.

Bisque of Lobsters.

This soup is made exactly like the *purée* of string-beans, with the veal stock and thickened cream, except that, in place of the string-bean pulp, the soup is now flavored and colored with the coral of lobster, dried in the oven, and pounded fine. This gives it a beautiful pink color. Little dice of the boiled lobster are then to be added. The lobster-dice may or may not be marinated before they are added to the soup, *i. e.*, sprinkled with a mixture of one table-spoonful of oil, three table-spoonfuls of vinegar, pepper, and salt, and left for two or three hours in the marinade. Season the soup with pepper and salt.

FISH.

If a fish is not perfectly fresh, perfectly cleaned, and thoroughly cooked, it is not eatable. It should be cleaned or drawn as soon as it comes from market, then put on the ice until the time of cooking. It should not be soaked, for it impairs the flavor, unless it is frozen, when it should be put into ice-cold water to thaw; or unless it is a salted fish, when it may be soaked overnight.

The greatest merit of a fish is freshness. The secret of the excellence of the fish at the Saratoga Lake House, where they have famous trout dinners, is that, as they are raised on the premises, they go almost immediately from the pond to the fish-kettle. One is to be pitied who has not tasted fish at the sea-shore, where fishermen come in just before dinner, with baskets filled with blue-fish, flounders, etc., fresh from the water.

A long, oval fish-kettle (page 52) is very convenient for frying or boiling fish. It has a strainer to fit, in which the fish is placed, enabling it to be taken from the kettle without breaking. A fish is sufficiently cooked when the meat separates easily from the bones. When the fish is quite done, it should be left no longer in the kettle; it will lose its flavor.

It makes a pleasant change to cook fish *"au gratin."* It is a simple operation, but little attempted in America. I would recommend this mode of cooking for eels, or the Western white-fish.

A fish is most delicious fried in olive-oil. A friend told me he purchased olive-oil by the keg, for cooking purposes. It is, of course, expensive, and lard or beef drippings answer very well. I would recommend, also, frying fish by *immersion.*

If a fish is to be served whole, do not cut off the head and tail. It also presents a better appearance to stand the fish on its belly rather than lay it on its side.

To Boil Fish.

All fish but salmon (which is put into warm water to preserve its color) should be placed in salted *cold* water, with a little vinegar or lemon-juice in it, to boil. It should then boil *very, very* gently, or the outside will break before the inside is done. It requires a little experience to know exactly how long to boil a fish. It must never be underdone; yet it must be taken from the water as soon as it is thoroughly done, or it will become insipid, watery, and colorless. It will require about eight minutes to the pound for large, thick fish, and about five minutes to the pound for thin fish, after the water begins to simmer, using only enough water to cover it. When done, drain it well before the fire. The fresh-water, or any kind of fish which have no decided flavor, are much better boiled *au court bouillon,* or with onions and carrots (sliced), parsley, two or three cloves, pepper, salt, vinegar, or wine—any or all of these added to the water. The sea-fish, or such as have a flavor *prononcé,* can be boiled in simple salted and acidulated water.

If you have no fish-kettle, and wish to boil a fish, arrange it in a circle on a plate, with an old napkin around it: when it is done, it can be carefully lifted from the kettle by the cloth, so that it will not be broken. When cuts of fish are boiled, you allow the water to just come to a boil; then remove the kettle to the back of the range, so that it will only simmer.

Always serve a sauce with a boiled fish, such as drawn butter, egg, caper, pickle, shrimp, oyster, *Hollandaise,* or piquante sauce.

To Boil Au Court Bouillon.

Among professional cooks, a favorite way of boiling a fish is in water saturated with vegetables, called *court bouillon*; consequently, a fish cooked in this manner would be called, for instance, "Pike, *au court bouillon.*" It is rather a pity this way of cooking has a French name; however, if one is not unduly scared at that, one can see how simple it is.

Dubois's Receipt.—Mince a carrot, an onion, and a small piece of celery; fry them in a little butter, in a stew-pan; add some parsley, some peppercorns, and three or four cloves. Now pour on two quarts of hot water and a pint of vinegar. Let it boil a quarter of an hour; skim it, salt it, and use it for boiling the fish.

It is improved by using white or red wine instead of vinegar; only use then three parts of wine to one of water. These stocks are easily preserved, and may be used several times.

To boil the fish: Rub the fish with lemon-juice and salt, put it in a kettle, and cover it with *court bouillon.* Let it only simmer, not boil hard, until thoroughly done. Serve the fish on a napkin, surrounded with parsley. Serve a caper, pickle, or any kind of fish sauce, in a sauce-boat.

To Fry Fish.

By frying fish I mean that it is to be *immersed* in hot lard, beef drippings, or olive-oil. Let there be a little more fat than will cover the fish; otherwise it is liable to stick to the bottom and burn. Do not put in the fish until the fat is tested, and found to be quite hot. If the fat were not hot enough, the fish would absorb some of it, making it greasy and unwholesome. If it is hot enough, the fish will absorb nothing at all.

To prepare fish for frying, dredge them first with flour; then brush them with beaten egg, and roll them in fine or sifted bread, or cracker crumbs. When they are browned on one side, turn them over in the hot fat. When done, let them drain quite dry.

Cutlets of any large fish are particularly nice egged and bread-crumbed, fried, and served with tomato sauce or slices of lemon.

Fish Fried in Batter.

Cut almost any kind of fish in fillets or pieces one-fourth of an inch thick, and one or two inches square; only be careful to have them all of the same shape and size. Sprinkle them with pepper and salt, and roll each one in batter (No. 2, page 98). Fry them in boiling lard. Arrange them tastefully in a circle, one overlapping the other. Garnish with fresh or fried parsley. Potatoes *à la Parisienne* may be piled in the centre, and *sauce Tartare* (see page 128) served separately in a sauce-boat.

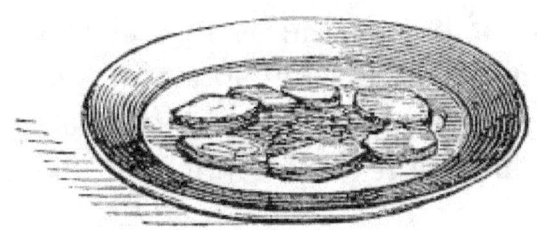

To Broil Fish.

The same rule applies to broiling fish as to every thing else. If the fish is small, it requires a clear, hot fire. If the fish is large, the fire must be moderate; otherwise the outside of the fish would be burned before the inside is cooked. Many rub the fish over with olive-oil; others split a large fish; still others broil it whole, and cut notches at equal distances across its sides. When you wish to turn the fish, separate carefully with a knife any part of it which sticks to the gridiron; then, holding a platter over the fish with one hand, turn the gridiron over with the other, leaving the fish on the platter: it will now be a more easy matter to turn it without breaking. As soon as the fish is done, sprinkle over pepper and salt, and spread butter all over it with a knife. Set it in the oven a moment, so that the butter may soak in the fish. This is the most common way of seasoning it. It is almost as easy to first sprinkle pepper and salt, then a few drops of lemon-juice, over the fish; then a table-spoonful of parsley, chopped fine; then some melted butter over all. Put it a moment in the oven to soak. They call this a *maître-d'hôtel* sauce. Quite simple, is it not? It is especially nice for a broiled shad.

To Bake Fish.

When cleaning the fish, do not cut off the head and tail. Stuff it. Two or three receipts are given for the stuffing. Sew it, or confine the stuffing by winding the cord several times around the fish. Lay several pieces of pork, cut in strings, across the top; sprinkle over water, pepper, salt, and bread-crumbs; put some hot water into the pan; bake in a hot oven, *basting very often*. When done (the top should be nicely browned), serve a sauce with it. The best fishes to bake are white-fish, blue-fish, shad, etc. If not basted very often, a baked fish will be very dry. For this reason, an ordinary cook should never bake a fish. I believe, however, they never cook them in any other way.

STUFFINGS FOR FISH.

Bread Stuffing.

Soak half a pound of bread-crumbs in water; when the bread is soft, press out all the water. Fry two table-spoonfuls of minced onion in some butter; add the bread, some chopped parsley, a table-spoonful of chopped suet, and pepper and salt. Let it cook a moment; take it off the fire, and add an egg.

Meat Stuffing.

This stuffing is best made with veal, and almost an equal quantity of bacon chopped fine. Put in a quarter of its volume of white softened bread-crumbs, pressed out well; add a little chopped onion, parsley, or mushrooms; season highly.

If the fish should be baked with wine, this dressing can be used, viz.:

Soak about three slices of bread. When the water is well pressed out, season it with salt, a little cayenne, a little mace, and moisten it with port-wine or sherry; add the juice and the grated rind of half a lemon.

To Bake a Fish with Wine (*Mrs. Samuel Treat*).

Stuff a fish with the following dressing. Soak some bread in water, squeeze it dry, and add an egg well beaten. Season it with pepper, salt, and a little parsley or thyme; grease the baking-pan (one just the right size for holding the fish) with butter; season the fish on top, and put it into the pan with about two cups of boiling water; baste it well, adding more boiling water when necessary. About twenty minutes before serving, pour over it a cup of sour wine, and a small piece of butter (Mrs. Treat adds also two or three table-spoonfuls of Worcestershire sauce mixed with the wine—of course, this may be left out if more convenient); put half a lemon, sliced, into the gravy; baste the fish again well. When it is thoroughly baked, remove it from the pan; garnish the top with the slices of lemon; finish the sauce in the baking-dish by adding a little butter rubbed to a paste in some flour; strain, skim, and serve it in a sauce-boat.

To Stew Fish, or Fish en Matelote.

Cut the fish transversely into pieces about an inch or an inch and a half long; sprinkle salt on them, and let them remain while you boil two or three onions (sliced) in a very little water; pour off this water when the onions are cooked, and add to them pepper, about a tea-cupful of hot water, and a tea-cupful of wine if it is claret or white wine, and two or three table-spoonfuls if it is sherry or port: now add the fish. When it begins to simmer, throw in some little balls of butter which have been rolled in flour. When the fish is thoroughly cooked, serve it very hot. This is a very good manner of cooking any fresh-water fish.

Fish is much better stewed with some wine. Of course, it is quite possible to stew fish without it, in which case add a little parsley.

To Cook Fish au Gratin.

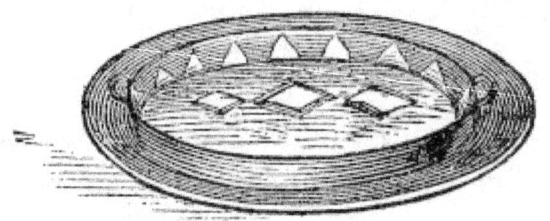

This is a favorite manner with the French of cooking fish. The fish is served in the same dish in which it is cooked. It is called a *gratin* dish—generally an oval silver-plated platter, or it may be of block-tin. A fish *au gratin* is rather expensive, on account of the mushrooms; however, the French canned mushrooms (*champignons*) are almost as good as fresh ones, and are much cheaper.

Receipt.—First put into a saucepan butter size of an egg, then a handful of shallots, or one large onion minced fine; let it cook ten minutes, when mix in half a cupful of flour; then mince three-fourths of a cupful of mushrooms. Add a tea-cupful of hot water (or better, stock) to the saucepan, then a glass of white or red wine, salt, and pepper. After mixing them well, add the minced mushrooms and a little minced parsley. Skin the fish, cut off the head and tail, split it in two, laying bare the middle bone; slip the knife under the bone, removing it smoothly. Now cut the fish in pieces about an inch long. Moisten the *gratin* dish with butter, arrange the cuts of fish tastefully on it, pour over the sauce, then sprinkle the whole with bread-crumbs which have been dried and grated. Put little pieces of butter over all, and bake. The dish may be garnished with little diamonds of fried or toasted and buttered bread around the edge. Or,

This is a pretty dish *au gratin*: Put mashed potatoes (which must be still hot when arranged) in a circle on the outside of the *gratin* dish, then a row of the pieces of fish (which have been cooked as just described) around the middle of the dish, or just inside the potatoes. Put some mashed potatoes also in the middle of the dish. Garnish here and there with mushrooms. Pour the sauce just described and bread-crumbs over the fish, and bake five or ten minutes.

Fish à la Crème (*Mrs. Audenreid*).

Boil a fish weighing four pounds in salted water. When done, remove the skin, and flake it, leaving out the bones. Boil one quart of rich milk. Mix butter size of a small egg with three table-spoonfuls of flour, and stir it smoothly in the milk, adding also two or three sprigs of parsley and half an onion chopped fine, a little Cayenne pepper, and salt. Stir it over the fire until it has thickened.

Butter a *gratin* dish. Put in first a layer of fish, then of dressing, and continue in alternation until all the fish is used, with dressing on top. Sprinkle sifted bread-crumbs over the top. Bake half an hour. Garnish with parsley and slices of hard-boiled egg.

As the rules for boiling, broiling, frying, cooking *au gratin*, and stewing are the same for nearly all kinds of fish, I will not repeat the receipts for each particular one. I will only suggest the best manner for cooking certain kinds, and will add certain receipts not under the general rule:

SALMON

is undoubtedly best boiled. The only exception to the rule of boiling fish is in the case of salmon, which must be put in hot instead of cold water, to preserve its color. A favorite way of boiling a whole salmon is in the form of a letter S, as in plate. It is done as follows: Thread a trussing-needle with some twine; tie the end of the string around the head, fastening it tight; then pass the needle through the centre part of the body, draw the string tight, and fasten it around the tail. The fish will assume the desired form.

For parties or evening companies, salmon boiled in this form (middle cuts are also used), served cold, with a *Mayonnaise* sauce poured over, is a favorite dish. It is then generally mounted in style, on an oval or square block pedestal, three or four inches high, made of bread (two or three days old), called a *croustade*, carved in any form with a sharp knife. It is then fried a light-brown in boiling lard. Oftener these *croustades* are made of wood, which are covered with white paper, and brushed over with a little half-set aspic jelly. The salmon is then decorated with squares of aspic jelly.

A decoration of quartered hard-boiled eggs or of cold cauliflower-blossoms is very pretty, and is palatable also with the *Mayonnaise* sauce. The best sauces for a boiled salmon served hot are the *sauce Hollandaise*, lobster, shrimp, or oyster sauces—the *sauce Hollandaise* being the favorite.

If lobster sauce is used, the coral of the lobster is dried, and sprinkled over the fish, reserving some with which to color the sauce, as in receipt for lobster sauce (see page 122).

If shrimp sauce is used, some whole shrimps should be saved for decorating the dish.

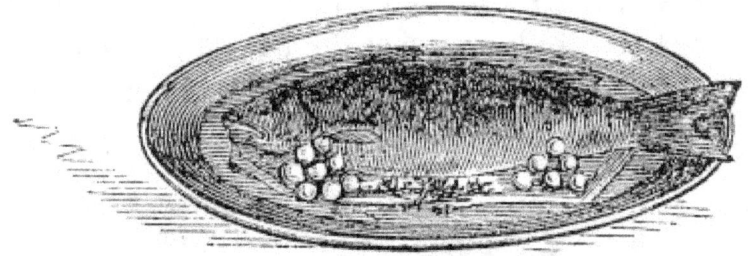

In decorating salmon, as well as any other kind of fish, potatoes cut in little balls, and placed like little piles of cannon-balls around the dish, are pretty. The potatoes should be simply boiled in salted water. An alternate pile of button mushrooms are pretty, and good also. Parsley or any pretty leaves around a dish always give a fresh and tasteful appearance. Or,

An exceedingly pretty garnish for a large fish is one of smelts (in rings, see receipt, page 111) fried in boiling lard. In this case, add slices of lemon. Still another pretty garnish is of fried oysters or fried parsley, or both.

It is quite appropriate to serve a middle cut of salmon at a dinner: 1st, because it is the best cut; 2d, because it is easier and cheaper to serve; and, 3d, because one never cares to supply more than is necessary. This cut is better slowly boiled, also, in the acidulated salted water.

To Broil Salmon.

Take two slices of salmon cut from the middle of the fish, sprinkle over a little lemon-juice, Cayenne pepper, salt, and salad-oil. Let it then remain for half an hour. Rub the gridiron well with beef-suet or pork. As it is a nice matter to broil salmon without burning, it would be well to wrap it in buttered or oiled paper just before broiling. Serve a *maître-d'hôtel*, pickle, caper, anchovy, or a horse-radish sauce.

SALMON CUTLETS.

Remove the skin and bone from some slices of salmon one-third of an inch thick; trim them into cutlet shape; sprinkle on pepper, salt, and flour, and dip them into beaten eggs mixed with a little chopped parsley or onion; then bread-crumb them. Fry them in boiling lard. This is the better way, or they may be fried or *sautéd* in butter in a *sauté* pan. Arrange the pieces one over the other in a circle. Pour a pickle, or *Tartare* sauce, in the centre.

SLICES OF SALMON BOILED.

If a family is small, and it should not be advisable to buy a large middle cut of salmon, it would be preferable to buy, for instance, two slices. Boil them very slowly in acidulated salted water, or in the *court bouillon* with wine. Serve them with parsley between, and a napkin underneath. Serve a *sauce Hollandaise* in the sauce-boat.

CANNED SALMON.

The California canned salmon is undoubtedly one of the greatest successes in canning. By keeping a few cans in the house, one is always ready in any emergency to produce a fine dish of salmon in a few minutes. It is particularly nice for a breakfast-dish, heated, seasoned with pepper and salt, placed on thin slices of buttered toast, with a cream dressing poured over all, *i. e.*, milk thickened on the fire, by stirring it into a *roux* (see page 51) of butter and flour, and seasoned with pepper, salt, and a few pieces of fresh butter just before serving. For dinner it is excellent served with any of the fish sauces. Salmon is also nice served in shells, as for trout (see page 109).

SHAD.

This delicious fish is undoubtedly best broiled, with a *maître-d'hôtel* sauce; but it is good also cut in slices, and *sautéd*.

TROUT.

If large, they may be broiled, boiled, or baked. If boiled or broiled, serve the *sauce Hollandaise* with them. Professional cooks generally boil it in the *court bouillon*. Smaller trout are better egged, rolled in salted corn-meal, and thrown into boiling lard.

The trout is a very nice fish for an *au gratin*, or stewed, called then *en matelote*.

Trout in Cases or in Shells (*en Coquilles*).

Parboil little trout; cut the fish into pieces about an inch long, or into dice; place them in paper cases (which have been buttered or oiled, and placed in the oven a few moments to harden the paper so as to enable it to hold the sauce). After partly filling the cases with the pieces of fish, pour over them some fine herb sauce (see page 128), and sprinkle over bread-crumbs; put them into the oven twenty minutes before dinner to bake.

If shells are used, little plated-silver ones (scallop shells) are preferable. In that case, it would be better to fry the fish (seasoned with pepper, salt, and a little lemon-juice) in a *sauté* pan; cut them in dice afterward, and put them in the shells; pour over a fine herb or a Bechamel sauce; strew the top with grated bread-crumbs; place them a few moments in the oven to brown the tops, and serve.

COD-FISH.

Fresh cod-fish is better boiled. The fish is so large that it is generally boiled in slices. After it is well salted, horse-radish and vinegar in the boiling water will improve the fish. Oyster-sauce is the favorite sauce for a boiled cod-fish. Capers might be mixed with the oyster-sauce. Some serve the fish with the sauce poured over it. Any of the fish sauces may be served with fresh cod-fish. These slices may also be broiled and served with a *maître-d'hôtel* sauce, or they may be egged and bread-crumbed, and fried in boiling lard.

Crimped Cod-fish (*Rudmanii*).

Soak two slices of cod-fish one inch thick for two hours in ice-water; put them into the stew-pan, and, pouring over enough salted boiling water to cover them, let them *simmer* for about ten minutes; place them neatly on a platter on a folded napkin, garnish with parsley, and pour into the two cavities a *Tartare* or a pickle sauce.

Salt Cod-fish.

Soak this in water overnight; parboil it, changing the water once or twice; separate the flakes. Serve them on thin slices of toast, with an egg sauce poured over. Or,

Mince it when boiled in very little water, which should be changed once; thicken it with butter and flour mixed; cook about two minutes, then break in several eggs. When the eggs are cooked and mixed with the fish, pour all on thin slices of buttered toast.

Cod-fish Balls.

Cut the cod-fish in pieces; soak them about an hour in lukewarm water, when the bones and skin may be easily removed; pull the fish then into fine shreds, and put it on the stove in some cold water. As soon as it begins to boil, change the water, and repeat this process a second time. It is not proper to boil it, as it renders it tough. As soon as the fish is ready, some potatoes must be cooked at the same time, *i. e.*, boiled tender, and well-mashed while still hot, with a little butter added. Mix half as much cod-fish as potatoes while both are *still hot*. Form them into little balls or thick flat cakes. Fry them in a little hot butter in a *sauté* pan, or immerse them in boiling-hot lard. It makes all the difference in the flavor of the balls if the fish and potatoes are mixed while both are *hot*. Of course, they are better fried at once, but may be made the night before serving (at breakfast), if they are only properly *mixed*.

Fish Chowder.

Cut three pounds of any kind of fresh fish (cod-fish is especially good), one and a half pounds of potatoes, and one large onion (three ounces) into slices; also, half a pound of salt pork into half-inch squares or dice.

Put the pork and onions into a saucepan, and fry them a light brown; then add a cupful of claret; and when it boils take it from the fire.

Butter a large stew-pan, and put in first a layer of potatoes, then a layer of fish, then a sprinkle of onions and pork (strained from the claret), pepper and salt, and continue these alternations until it is all in, having the potatoes on top. Now pour the claret over the top, and barely cover the whole with boiling water. Cover closely, and let it simmer for fifteen minutes without disturbing it.

In the mean time, bring a pint of milk (or, better, cream) to a boil, take it from the fire, and cut into it three ounces of butter, and break in three ship-crackers. Arrange the slices of fish and potatoes in the shape of a dome in the centre of a hot platter. Place the softened crackers (skimmed from the milk) over the top, and pour over the milk. Serve very hot.

SMALL PAN-FISH (*Perch, Sun-fish, etc.*).

They are generally preferred peppered, salted, then rolled in salted corn-meal, and fried either in a *sauté* pan with a little lard and some slices of pork, or in boiling lard. They make also a good stew *en matelote*, or a good *au gratin*. Their chief excellence consists in their being perfectly fresh, and served hot.

MACKEREL

should be broiled, and served *à la maître-d'hôtel*.

SMELTS

are good salted, peppered, and rolled in salted corn-meal or flour, and fried in boiling-hot lard, but better egged and bread-crumbed before frying. They should be served *immediately*, or they will lose their crispness and flavor. When served as a garnish for a large fish, they should be fried in the shape of rings. This is easily done by putting the tail of the fish into its mouth, and holding it with a pin. After it is fried, the pin is withdrawn, as the fried fish will hold its shape. Place these rings around the fish, with an additional garnish of parsley and lemon slices; or the rings may be served alone in a circle around the side of a platter, with a tomato or a *Tartare* sauce in the centre.

There can be no prettier manner of serving them alone than one often seen in Paris. They are fried in the usual manner; then a little silver or silver-plated skewer four inches long is drawn through two or three of the smelts, running it carefully through the eyes. One skewerful, with a slice of lemon on top, is served for each person at table. If the silver-plated skewers are too extravagant, little ones of polished wire will answer.

Fried Slices of Fish, with Tomato Sauce (*Fish à l'Orlay*).

Bone and skin the fish, and cut it into even slices; or if a flounder or any flat fish is used, begin at the tail, and, keeping the knife close to the bone, separate each side of the fish neatly from it; then cut each side in two, lengthwise, leaving the fish in four long pieces. Remove the skin carefully. After having sprinkled pepper and salt over them, roll each piece first in sifted cracker or bread crumbs, then in half a cupful of milk mixed with an egg, and then in the crumbs again. They are better fried in a *sauté* pan in a little hot butter; yet they may be *sautéd* in a little hot lard, with some neat slices of pork, or fried in boiling lard.

Pour tomato sauce No. 2 (see page 125) on a hot platter, arrange the pieces of fish symmetrically on it, and serve immediately.

To Fry Eels.

Skin them, cut them into four-inch lengths, season them with salt and pepper, roll them in flour or salted corn-meal, and fry them in boiling lard. Some parboil eels and bull-heads, saying it removes a muddy taste. I do not think it is necessary. Fried eels are generally served with a tomato, a pickle, or a *Tartare* sauce.

Eels Stewed (*London Cooking-school*).

Put three-quarters of a cupful of butter into a stew-pan; when hot, add four small onions minced fine, which cook to a light-brown color; add then a table-spoonful of flour; when well mixed and cooked, add two cupfuls of stock, a wine-glassful of port-wine, and two bay leaves (the bay leaves may be omitted). Now put in the eels (two small ones or one large one), cut into pieces one inch long. Cover tightly.

They will be ready to send to the table in about fifteen minutes, served on a hot platter, with a circle around them of toasted or fried slices of bread (*croûtons*), cut diamond-shaped.

SHELL-FISH.

OYSTERS.

Raw Oysters.

Drain them well in a colander, marinate them, *i. e.*, sprinkle over plenty of pepper and salt, and let them remain in a cold place for at least half an hour before serving. This makes a great difference in their flavor. They may be served in the half-shell with quarters or halves of lemons in the same dish. I think a prettier arrangement is to serve them in a block of ice. Select a ten-pound block; melt with a hot flat-iron a symmetrical-shaped cavity in the top to hold the oysters; chip also from the sides at the base, so that the ice-block may stand in a large platter on the napkin. When the oysters are well salted and peppered, place them in the ice, and let them remain in some place where the ice will not melt until the time of serving. The salt will help to make the oysters very cold. The ice may be decorated with leaves or smilax vines, and a row of lemon quarters or halves may be placed around the platter at the base of the ice. It has an especially pretty effect served on a table by gas-light. The English often serve little thin squares of buttered brown bread (like Boston brown bread) with oysters.

Fried Oysters.

Drain the oysters in the colander; sprinkle over pepper and salt, which mix well with them, and put them in a cold place for fifteen or twenty minutes before cooking. This is marinating them. When ready to cook, roll each one first in sifted cracker-crumbs, then in beaten egg mixed with a little milk and seasoned with pepper and salt, then in the cracker-crumbs again. You will please remember the routine: *first*, the crumbs before the egg, as the egg will not adhere well to the oyster without the crumbs; now throw them into boiling-hot lard (as you would fry doughnuts), first testing to see if it is hot enough. As soon as they assume a light-brown color they should be drained, and served immediately on a hot platter.

Oysters should not be fried until the persons at table are ready to eat them, as it takes only a few moments to fry them, and they are not good unless very hot.

The platter of oysters may be garnished with a table-spoonful of chopped pickles or chowchow placed at the four opposite sides; or the oysters may be served as a border around cold slaw (see receipt, page 224), when they are an especially nice course for dinner; or they may be served with celery, either plain or in salad. As the platter for the fried oysters is hot, the celery salad or cold slaw might be piled on a folded napkin in the centre.

Scalloped Oysters in Shells.

They may be served cooked in their shells, or in silver scallop shells, when they present a better appearance than when cooked and served all in one dish.

If cooked in an oyster or clam shell, one large, or two or three little oysters are placed in it, with a few drops of the oyster liquor. It is sprinkled with pepper and salt, and cracker or bread crumbs. Little pieces of butter are placed over the top. When all are ready, they are put into the oven. When they are plump and hot, they are done. Brown the tops with a salamander, or with a red-hot kitchen shovel.

If they are cooked in the silver scallop shells, which are larger, several oysters are served in the one shell; one or two are put in, peppered, salted, strewed with cracker-crumbs and small pieces of butter; then more layers, until the shell is full, or until enough are used for one person. Moisten them with the oyster-juice, and strew little pieces of butter over the top. They are merely kept in the oven until they are thoroughly hot, then browned with a salamander. Serve one shell for each person at table, placed on a small plate. The oysters may be bearded or not.

Scalloped Oysters.

Ingredients: Three dozen oysters, a large tea-cupful of bread or cracker crumbs, two ounces of fresh butter, pepper and salt, half a tea-cupful of oyster-juice.

Make layers of these ingredients, as described in the last article, in the top of a chafing-dish, or in any kind of pudding or *gratin* dish; bake in a quick oven about fifteen minutes; brown with a salamander.

Oyster Stew.

Put a quart of oysters on the fire in their own liquor. The moment they *begin* to boil, skim them out, and add to the liquor a half-pint of hot cream, salt, and Cayenne pepper to taste. Skim it well, take it off the fire, add to the oysters an ounce and a half of butter broken into small pieces. Serve immediately.

Oyster Soup (see page 93).

Oyster or Clam Fritters.

Oysters served on buttered toast for breakfast, or in *vols-au-vent*, silver scallop-shells, or in paper boxes, are very nice made after the receipts on page 241. They or the fricasseed oysters may be served in either of the above ways.

Fricassee of Oysters (*Oysters à la Boulette*).

Put one quart, or twenty-five, oysters on the fire in their own liquor. The moment it begins to boil, turn it into a hot dish through a colander, leaving the oysters in the colander. Put into the saucepan two ounces of butter (size of an egg), and when it bubbles sprinkle in one ounce (a table-spoonful) of sifted flour; let it cook a minute without taking color, stirring it well with a wire egg-whisk; then add, mixing well, a cupful of the oyster liquor. Take it from the fire and mix in the yolks of two eggs, a little salt, a very little Cayenne pepper, one tea-spoonful of lemon-juice, and one grating of nutmeg. Beat it well; then return it to the fire to set the eggs, without allowing it to boil. Put in the oysters.

These oysters may be served on thin slices of toast for breakfast or tea, or in papers (*en papillote*), or as a filling for patties for dinner.

To Roast Canned Oysters.

Drain them. Put them in a spider which is very hot; turn them in a moment, so that they may cook on both sides. It only takes a few seconds to cook them. Put them on a hot plate in which there are pepper, salt, and a little hot melted butter. They should be served immediately. They have the flavor of the oyster roasted in the shell.

Some cook them in this manner at table on a chafing-dish by means of the spirit-lamp.

Spiced Oysters (*Miss Lestlie*).

Ingredients: Two hundred oysters, one pint of vinegar, a nutmeg grated, eight blades of whole mace, three dozen whole cloves, one tea-spoonful of salt, two tea-spoonfuls of whole allspice, and as much Cayenne pepper as will lie on the point of a knife.

Put the oysters with their liquor into a large earthen vessel; add to them the vinegar and all the other ingredients. Stir all well together and set them over a slow fire, keeping them covered. Stir them to the bottom several times. As soon as they are well scalded, they are done. To be eaten cold.

CLAMS.

CLAMS COOKED WITH CREAM (*Mrs. Audenreid*).

Chop fifty small clams not too fine, and season them with pepper and salt. Put into a stew-pan butter the size of an egg, and when it bubbles sprinkle in a tea-spoonful of flour, which cook a few moments; stir gradually into it the clam liquor, then the clams, which stew about two or three minutes; then add a cupful of boiling cream, and serve immediately. The clams may or may not be bearded.

CLAM CHOWDER.

Put fifty clams on the fire in their own liquor, with a little salt. When they have boiled about three minutes, strain them, and return the liquor to the fire. Chop a medium-sized onion (two ounces) into small pieces, and cut six ounces of pork into dice. Fry both a light color in two ounces (size of an egg) of butter; then stir in three ounces of flour (two table-spoonfuls). When thoroughly cooked, add the clam liquor, half a pint of good stock or milk, the same quantity of cream, a salt-spoonful of mace, a salt-spoonful of thyme, salt to taste, and eight ounces of potatoes cut into dice. When these are cooked, and the chowder is about to be sent to table, add the clams cut in dice, and four ounces of ship-bread or crackers broken in pieces.

TUNISON CLAM CHOWDER.

Ingredients: Two hundred soft clams, one large onion, twenty large crackers, can of tomatoes, parsley (chopped fine), half a pound of butter, one large tea-spoonful of sweet marjoram, thyme, sage, savory, half a tea-spoonful of ground cloves, and half a tea-spoonful of curry.

Boil well; then add half a pint of milk and half a pint of sherry wine.

CLAM FRITTERS (see page 230).

CLAM SOUP (see page 93).

CRABS AND LOBSTERS.

SOFT-SHELL CRABS.

Dry them; sprinkle them with pepper and salt; roll them, first in flour, then in egg (half a cupful of milk mixed in one egg), then in cracker-dust, and fry them in boiling lard.

DEVILED CRAB.

When the crabs are boiled, take out the meat and cut it into small pieces (dice); clean well the shells.

To six ounces of crab meat, mix two ounces of bread-crumbs, two hard-boiled eggs chopped, the juice of half a lemon, Cayenne pepper and salt. Mix all with cream or cream sauce, or, what is still better, a Bechamel sauce (see page 127). Fill the shells with the mixture, smooth the tops, sprinkle over sifted bread-crumbs, and color it in a quick oven.

DEVILED LOBSTER

is made in the same way as deviled crab, merely substituting the lobster for the crab, and adding a grating of nutmeg to the seasoning. In boiling lobsters and crabs, they are sufficiently cooked when they assume a bright-red color. Too much boiling renders them tough.

LOBSTER CHOPS.

Cut half a pound of the flesh of a boiled lobster into small dice. Put two ounces of butter into a stew-pan, and when it bubbles sprinkle in two ounces of flour (one table-spoonful). Cook it; then pour in a cupful of boiling cream and the lobster dice. Stir it until it is scalding hot; then take it from the fire, and, when slightly cooled, stir in the beaten yolks of three eggs, a grating of nutmeg, a little Cayenne pepper, and salt to taste. Return the mixture to the fire, and stir it long enough to well set the eggs.

Butter a platter, on which spread the lobster mixture half an inch deep. When cold, form it into the shape of chops, pointed at one end; bread-crumb, egg, and crumb them again, and fry them in boiling lard. Stick a claw into the end of each lobster chop after it is cooked.

Place the chops in a circle, overlapping each other, on a napkin. Decorate the dish by putting the tail of the lobster in the centre, and its head, with the long horns, on the tail. Around the outside of the circle of chops arrange the legs, cut an inch each side of the middle joints, so that they will form two equal sides of a triangle.

A Good Way to Prepare a Lobster.

Put into a saucepan butter the size of a small egg, and a tea-spoonful of minced onion. When it has cooked, sprinkle in a tea-spoonful of flour, which cook also; then stir in one cupful of the water in which the lobster was boiled, one cupful of milk, one cupful of strong veal or beef stock, pepper, and salt: add the meat of the boiled lobster, and when quite hot pour all in the centre of a hot platter. Decorate the dish with the lobster's head in the centre, fried-bread diamonds (*croûtons*) around the outside; or in any prettier way you choose, with the abundant resources of lobster legs and trimmings.

FROGS.

Frogs are such a delicacy that it is a pity not to prepare them with care.

The hind legs only are used. They may be made into a broth the same as chicken broth, and are considered a very advantageous diet for those suffering with pulmonary affections.

Frogs Fried.

Put them in salted boiling water, with a little lemon-juice, and boil them three minutes; wipe them; dip them first in cracker-dust, then in eggs (half a cupful of milk mixed in two eggs and seasoned with pepper and salt), then again in cracker-crumbs. When they are all breaded, clean off the bone at the end with a dry cloth. Put them in a wire basket and dip them in boiling lard, to fry. Put a little paper (see page 61) on the end of each bone; place them on a hot platter, in the form of a circle, one overlapping the other, with French pease in the centre. Serve immediately, while they are still crisp and hot.

SAUCES.

The French say the English only know how to make one kind of sauce, and a poor one at that. Notwithstanding the French understand the sauce question, it is very convenient to make the drawn butter, and, by adding different flavorings, make just so many kinds of sauce. For instance, by adding capers, shrimps, chopped pickles, anchovy paste, chopped boiled eggs, lobster, oysters, parsley, cauliflower, etc., one has caper, shrimp, pickle, anchovy, egg, and the other sauces. The drawn-butter sauce is simple, yet few make it properly, managing generally to have it insipid, and with flour uncooked. If a housekeeper has any pride about having a good table, she will be amply repaid for learning some of the French sauces, which are, at last, simple enough. We are often frightened to see many items in a receipt; we shake our heads dubiously at the trouble and extravagance of one receipt mentioning thyme, nutmeg, bay-leaf, mace, shallot, capers, pepper-corns, parsley, and, last of all the horrors, stock. As far as the herbs are concerned, an investment of twenty-five cents will purchase enough mace, thyme, bay-leaves, and pepper-corns for a year's supply of abundant sauces, to say nothing of their uses for braising, *blanquettes*, etc. Five cents' worth of shallots should last a long time; they are sold in all city markets, being only young forced onions. Capers would be extravagant if a bottleful, costing sixty cents, would not last a year in a small-sized family. I have already said enough about stock to show that one must be very incompetent if a little of it can not be at hand, made of trimmings and cheap pieces of meat and bones.

The use of mushrooms and truffles, which are comparatively cheap in France, can not be extensively introduced here. A little tin can, holding about a gill of tasteless truffles, costs three or four dollars: however, mushrooms are much less expensive, and infinitely better. A can of mushrooms costs forty cents, and is sufficient for several sauces and *entrées*.

Some persons raise mushrooms in their cellars. A small, rich bed in a dark place where the soil will not freeze, planted with mushroom spawn, will yield enough mushrooms for the family, and the neighbors besides, with very little trouble and expense.

The French white sauces differ from the English white sauce, as they are made with strong white stock, prepared with veal, or chickens, or both, and some vegetables for a basis. If one would learn to make the *sauce Bechamel*, it will be found an easy affair to prepare many delicious *entrées*, such as chicken in shells (*en coquille*), or in papers (*en papillote*), and mushrooms in crust (*croûte aux champignons*).

For boiled fish the *sauce Hollandaise* is a decided success. In Paris every one speaks of this delicious sauce, and bribes the *chef de cuisine* for the receipt. It is made without stock, and is very simple.

For fried fish the perfection of accompaniments is the *sauce Tartare*—a mere addition of some capers, shallots, parsley, and pickles to the *sauce Mayonnaise*.

When tomatoes are so abundant, it is unpardonable that one should never serve a tomato sauce with a beefsteak, and a score of other meat dishes.

For a chicken or a lobster salad, learn unquestionably the *sauce Mayonnaise*.

In the thickening of sauces, let it be remembered that butter and flour should be well cooked together before the sauce is added, to prevent the flour from tasting uncooked. In butter sauces, however, only enough butter should be used to cook the flour, the remainder added, cut in pieces, after the sauce is taken from the fire. This preserves its flavor.

Drawn-butter Sauce.

Ingredients: Three ounces of butter, one ounce of flour, half a pint of water (or, better, white stock), and a pinch of salt and pepper.

Put two ounces of the butter into a stew-pan, and when it bubbles, sprinkle in the flour; stir it well with a wire egg-whisk until the flour is thoroughly cooked without taking color, and then mix in well the half-pint of water or stock. Take it off the fire, pass it through a sieve or gravy-strainer, and stir in the other ounce of butter cut in pieces. When properly mixed and melted, it is ready for use. This makes a pint of sauce.

Some persons like drawn-butter sauce slightly acid, in which case add a few drops of vinegar or lemon-juice just before serving.

Pickle Sauce.

Make a drawn-butter sauce; just before serving add two or three tablespoonfuls of pickled cucumbers chopped or minced very fine.

Boiled-egg Sauce.

Add to half a pint of drawn-butter sauce three hard-boiled eggs, chopped not too fine.

Caper Sauce.

Make a drawn-butter sauce—or, say, melt two ounces of butter in a saucepan; add a table-spoonful of flour; when the two are well mixed, add pepper and salt, and a little less than a pint of boiling water. Stir the sauce on the fire until it thickens, then add three table-spoonfuls of French capers. Removing the saucepan from the fire, stir into the sauce the yolk of an egg beaten with the juice of half a lemon.

Anchovy Sauce.

Add to half a pint of drawn-butter sauce two tea-spoonfuls of anchovy extract, or anchovy paste.

Shrimp Sauce.

To half a pint of drawn-butter sauce add one-third of a pint of picked boiled shrimps, whole, or chopped a little. Add at last moment a few drops of lemon-juice, and a very little Cayenne pepper. Let the sauce *simmer*, not boil. Some add a tea-spoonful of anchovy paste; more, perhaps, prefer it without the anchovy flavor.

Shrimps are generally sold at market already boiled. If they are not boiled, throw them into salted boiling water, and boil them until they are quite red. When cold, pick off the heads, and peel off the shells. Always save a few of the shrimps whole for garnishing the dish.

Lobster Sauce.

Before proceeding to make this sauce, break up the coral of the lobster, and put it on a paper in a slow oven for half an hour; then pound it in a mortar, and sprinkle it over the boiled fish when it is served. To prepare the sauce itself, chop the meat of the tail and claws of a good-sized lobster into pieces, not too small. Half an hour before dinner, make half a pint of drawn-butter sauce. Add to it the chopped lobster, a pinch of coral, a small pinch of Cayenne, and a little salt. An English lady says: "This process seems simple, yet nothing is rarer in cookery than good lobster sauce. The means of spoiling it are chiefly by chopping the lobster too small, or, worse, pounding it, inserting contents of the head, or using milk, or anchovy, or any sauces. It should not be a half-solid mass, or thin liquid, but the lobster should be distinct in a creamy bed."

Oyster Sauce.

Make a drawn-butter or white sauce; add a few drops of lemon or a table-spoonful of capers, or, if neither be at hand, a few drops of vinegar; add oysters strained from their liquor, and let them just come to a boil in the sauce.

This sauce is much better made with part cream, *i. e.*, used when making the drawn-butter sauce, instead of all water. In this case, do not add the lemon-juice or vinegar. Some make the white sauce of the oyster liquor, instead of water.

This sauce may be served in a sauce-boat, but it is nicer to pour it over the fish, boiled turkey, or chicken.

Parsley Sauce (*for Boiled Fish or Fowls*).

To half a pint of hot drawn-butter sauce add two table-spoonfuls of chopped parsley. The appearance of the sauce is improved by coloring it with a little spinach-green (see page 87).

Cauliflower Sauce (*for Boiled Poultry*).

Add boiled cauliflowers, cut into little flowerets, to a drawn-butter sauce made with part cream.

Lemon Sauce (*for Boiled Fowls*).

To half a pint of drawn-butter sauce add the inside of a lemon, chopped (seeds taken out), and the chicken liver boiled and mashed fine.

Chicken Sauce (*to serve with Boiled or Stewed Fowls*).

Put butter the size of an egg into a bright saucepan, and when it bubbles add a table-spoonful of flour; cook it, and add a pint, or rather less, of boiling water; when smooth, take it from the fire, and add the beaten yolks of two or three eggs, and a few drops of lemon-juice, pepper, and salt. Or, Stock can be used instead of boiling water, when two or three small slices of onion are placed in the butter after it begins to bubble, and then allowed to cook yellow; after the flour is cooked, stock is added instead of water, and when smooth, it is taken from the fire, a few drops of lemon-juice, pepper, and salt are added, and the sauce is strained through the gravy-strainer or sieve, to remove the pieces of onion.

Maître-d'hôtel Butter (*for Beefsteak, Broiled Meat, or Fish*).

Mix butter the size of an egg, the juice of half a lemon, and two or three sprigs of parsley, chopped very fine; pepper and salt all together. Spread this over any broiled meat or fish when hot; then put the dish into the oven a few moments, to allow the butter to penetrate the meat.

Mint Sauce (*for Roast Lamb*).

Put four table-spoonfuls of chopped mint, two table-spoonfuls of sugar, and a quarter of a pint of vinegar into the sauce-boat. Let it remain an hour or two before dinner, that the vinegar may become impregnated with the mint.

Currant-jelly Sauce (*for Venison*).

A simple sauce made of currant jelly melted with a little water is very nice; yet Francatelli's receipt is much better, viz.:

"Bruise half a stick of cinnamon and six cloves; put them into a stew-pan with one ounce of sugar and the peel of half a lemon, pared off very thin, and perfectly free from any portion of white pulp; moisten this with one and a half sherry-glassfuls of port-wine, and set the whole to gently simmer or heat on the stove for half an hour; then strain it into a small stew-pan containing half a glassful of currant jelly. Just before sending the sauce to the table, set it on the fire to boil, in order to melt the currant jelly, and so that it may mix with the essence of spice, etc."

Tomato Sauce (No. 1).

Stew six tomatoes half an hour with two cloves, a sprig of parsley, pepper, and salt; press this through a sieve; put a little butter into a saucepan over the fire, and when it bubbles add a heaping tea-spoonful of flour; mix and cook it well, and add the tomato-pulp, stirring until it is smooth and consistent.

Some add one or two slices of onion at first. It is a decided improvement to add three or four table-spoonfuls of stock; however, the sauce is very good without it, and people are generally too careless to have stock at hand.

Tomato Sauce (No. 2).

Ingredients: One-quart can of tomatoes, two cloves, one small sprig of thyme, two sprigs of parsley, half a small bay-leaf, three pepper-corns, three allspice, two slices of carrot (one and a half ounces), one-ounce onion (one small onion), one and a half ounces of butter (size of a pigeon's egg), one and a half ounces of flour (one table-spoonful).

Put the tomatoes over the fire with all the above ingredients but the butter and flour, and when they have boiled about twenty minutes strain them through a sieve. Make a *roux* by putting the butter into a stew-pan, and when it bubbles sprinkle in the flour, which let cook, stirring it well; then pour in the tomato-pulp; when it is well mixed, it is ready for use.

Sauce Hollandaise, or Dutch Sauce.

As this is one of the best sauces ever made for boiled fish, asparagus, or cauliflower, I will give two receipts. The first is Dubois'; the second is from the Cooking-school in New York. None should call themselves cooks unless they know how to make the *sauce Hollandaise*, and simple enough it is.

1st. "Pour four table-spoonfuls of good vinegar into a small stew-pan, and add some pepper-corns and salt; let the liquid boil until it is reduced to half; let it cool; then add to it the well-beaten yolks of four or five eggs, also four ounces (size of an egg) of good butter, more salt, if necessary, and a very little nutmeg. Set the stew-pan on a very slow fire, and stir the liquid until it is about as thick as cream; immediately remove it. Now put this stew-pan or cup into another pan containing a little warm water kept at the side of the fire. Work the sauce briskly with a spoon, or with a little whisk, so as to get it frothy, but adding little bits of butter, in all about three ounces" (*I* would say the size of half an egg). "When the sauce has become light and smooth, it is ready for use."

2d. "Put a piece of butter the size of a pigeon's egg into a saucepan, and when it bubbles stir in with an egg-whisk an even table-spoonful of flour; let it continue to bubble until the flour is thoroughly cooked, when stir in half a pint of boiling water, or, better, of veal stock; when it boils, take it from the fire, and stir into it gradually the beaten yolks of four eggs; return the sauce to the fire for a minute, to set the eggs, without allowing it to boil; again remove the sauce, stir in the juice of half a small lemon, and fresh butter the size of a walnut, cut into small pieces, to facilitate its melting, and stir all well with the whisk."

Mushrooms, for Garnish (*Gouffé*).

Separate the button part from the stalk; then peel them with a sharp knife, cutting off merely the skin. Put them into a stew-pan with a table-spoonful of lemon-juice and two table-spoonfuls of water. Toss them well, to impregnate them with the liquid. The object of the lemon-juice is to keep them white. Then put them on a sharp fire in boiling water, with some butter added. When they are boiled tender they are ready for use, *i. e.*, for garnishing and for sauces.

Mushroom Sauce (*to serve with Beefsteaks, Fillets of Beef, etc.*).

Having prepared the mushrooms by cutting off the stalks, and if they are large, by cutting them in halves or quarters, throw them into a little boiling water, or, what is much better, stock. Do not use more than is necessary to cover them. This must be seasoned with salt, pepper, and a little butter. Boil the mushrooms until they are tender, then thicken the gravy slightly with a *roux* of butter and flour. Add a few drops of lemon-juice. It is now ready to pour over the meat.

Mushroom White Sauce (*to serve with Boiled Fowls or with Cutlets*).

Prepare the mushrooms as for garnishing; boil them tender in rich white stock, made of veal or chicken; thicken with a *roux* of butter and flour, and add one or two table-spoonfuls of cream.

Mushroom Sauce (*made with Canned Mushrooms*).

Put a piece of butter the size of a walnut into a small stew-pan or tin basin, and when it bubbles add a tea-spoonful (not heaping) of flour; when well cooked, stir in a cupful of stock (reduced and strong), and half a tea-cupful of the mushroom-juice from the can; let it simmer for a minute or two; then, after straining it, add half or three quarters of a can of mushrooms, pepper, salt, and a few drops of lemon-juice. When thoroughly hot it is ready to pour over the meat.

A Simple Bechamel Sauce.

Put butter the size of a walnut into a stew-pan, and when it bubbles stir in an even table-spoonful of flour, which cook thoroughly without letting it take color. Mix into the *roux* a cupful of strong hot veal stock (*i. e.*, veal put into cold water and boiled four or five hours), a cupful of boiling cream, and one grating of nutmeg; let it simmer, stirring it well for a few minutes, then strain, and it is ready for use. The sauce would be improved if the usual soup-bunch vegetables were added to the stock while it is being made.

Bechamel Sauce.

Ingredients: One pint of veal stock (a knuckle of veal put into one gallon of cold water, boiled five hours, skimmed and strained), half an ounce of onion (quarter of a rather small one), quarter of an ounce of turnip (quarter of a turnip), one ounce of carrot (quarter of a good-sized carrot), half an ounce of parsley (two sprigs), quarter of a bay-leaf, half a sprig of thyme, three pepper-corns, half a lump of sugar, a small blade of mace.

Put one ounce (size of a walnut) of butter into a stew-pan, and when hot add to it all the above ingredients but the stock and the mace; fry this slowly until it assumes a yellow color; do not let it brown, as the sauce should be white when done; stir in now a table-spoonful (one ounce) of flour, which let cook a minute, and add the blade of mace and the stock (boiling) from another stew-pan. After it has all simmered about five minutes, strain it through a sieve without allowing the vegetables to pass through; return the strained sauce to the fire, reduce it by boiling about one-third, when add three or four table-spoonfuls of good thick cream, and the sauce is ready.

Sauce Aux Fines Herbes.

Ingredients: Half a pint of good stock, three table-spoonfuls of mushrooms, one table-spoonful of onions, two table-spoonfuls of parsley, and one shallot, all chopped fine. Fry the shallot and onion in a little butter until they assume a light-yellow color, then add a tea-spoonful of flour and cook it a minute; stir in the stock, mushrooms, and parsley, simmer for five minutes, then add a little Worcestershire sauce, and salt to taste. If no Worcestershire sauce is at hand, add pepper to taste in its place.

Sauce Tartare (*a Cold Sauce*).

To a scant half pint of *Mayonnaise* sauce (made with the mustard added) mix in two table-spoonfuls of capers, one small shallot (quarter of a rather small onion, a poor substitute), two gerkins (or two ounces of cucumber pickle), and one table-spoonful of parsley, all chopped *very* fine. This sauce will keep a long time, and is delicious for fried fish, fried oysters, boiled cod-fish, boiled tongue, or as dressing for a salad.

By making the following simple sauce, one can produce several by a little variation.

A Simple Brown Sauce.

Put into a saucepan a table-spoonful of minced onion and a little butter. When it has taken color, sprinkle in a heaping tea-spoonful of flour; stir well, and when brown add half a pint of stock. Cook it a few minutes, and strain. Now, by adding a cupful of claret, two cloves, a sprig of parsley, and one of thyme, a bay-leaf, pepper, and salt, and by boiling two or three minutes and straining it, one has the *sauce poivrade*.

If, instead of the claret, one should add to the *poivrade* sauce a table-spoonful each of minced cucumber pickles, vinegar, and capers, one has the *sauce piquante*.

By adding one tea-spoonful of made mustard, the juice of half a lemon, and a little vinegar to the *poivrade*, instead of the claret, one has the *sauce Robert*.